To my parents, Francis and Lucy

Theology and Religious Pluralism

The Challenge of Other Religions

GAVIN D'COSTA

Basil Blackwell

© Gavin D'Costa 1986

First published 1986

Basil Blackwell Ltd
108 Cowley Road, Oxford OX4 1JF, UK

Basil Blackwell Inc.
432 Park Avenue South, Suite 1505,
New York, NY 10016, USA

British Library Cataloguing in Publication Data
D'Costa, Gavin
  Theology and religious pluralism: the challenge
  of other religions.
  1. Christianity and other religions
  I. Title
  261.2   BR127

  ISBN 0–631–14517–6
  ISBN 0–631–14518–4 Pbk

Library of Congress Cataloging in Publication Data
D'Costa, Gavin, 1958–
  Theology and religious pluralism.

  Bibliography: p.
  Includes index.
  1. Christianity and other religions. I. Title
BR127.D4   1986   261.2   85–26730
ISBN 0–631–14517–6
ISBN 0–631–14518–4 (pbk.)

Typeset by Oxford Publishing Services, Oxford

Printed in Great Britain by Billing and Sons Ltd, Worcester

Contents

Acknowledgements

There are many people, more than I can mention, who have encouraged and supported me during the writing of this book. I especially wish to thank John Hick, Rowan Williams, Nicholas Lash, George Gispert-Sauch, Kenneth Cracknell, Ken Surin, Lesslie Newbigin, John Coventry, Alan Race, Paul Knitter, Nicky Slee and Chris Seville for reading sections of the initial draft. Their critical comments have always been helpful and stimulating. I also wish to thank my teaching colleagues Ken Oldfield, Maurice Lynch and, especially, Arthur Giles for arranging discussions of each chapter as it was being written. My thanks also to Julia Mosse of Basil Blackwell for her support. Finally, I must express my sincere gratitude for the patience and help of Beryl Gladstone and Gerard Loughlin, who went painstakingly through each chapter correcting poor expression and style, and made useful critical comments throughout. Needless to say, any deficiencies and inclarities that remain are entirely my own.

I also wish to thank the editors of *Modern Theology*, *New Blackfriars* and *The Modern Churchman* for allowing me to use material which has been published in their journals.

NOTE ON WORKS CITED

For full bibliographical details of works cited in the text and notes, the reader should refer to the bibliography at the end of the book. Titles frequently mentioned are shortened after the first reference. For works translated into English, the translation publication dates are given. Only the editions used are cited. Diacritical marks have been omitted to simplify the text. The Revised Standard Version of the Bible has been used for all biblical quotations.

CHAPTER 1

Introduction

An inscription on a monument to Captain Cook erected in 1827 near his birthplace at Marton, Yorkshire, proclaims 'that while it shall be deemed the honour of a Christian nation to spread Civilization and the blessings of the Christian faith among pagans and savage tribes, so long will the name of Captain Cook stand out among the most celebrated and most admired benefactors of the human race'. David Pailin has argued that British Christian attitudes to other religions ('pagan and savage tribes'), during the seventeenth and eighteenth centuries reflected a strong, confident, aggressive and often ill-informed type of Christianity.[1] A notable exception, providing a discordant note to the otherwise prevailing attitude of the time, was the distinguished orientalist, Sir William Jones. In his *Philosophy of the Asiaticks* (1794), he warned against the 'uncandid asperity' towards the wise men of ancient India, pointing out that three centuries before Christ, certain Indian texts contained the teaching that evil should be repaid with good. In later days Jones's discordant note and informed respect became an increasingly dominant theme in the debate concerning Christian attitudes to other religions.

Jones and Cook, each in their own way, were instrumental in initiating a now unavoidable *consciousness* by Christians that they inhabit a religiously pluralist world. I stress the word consciousness because the situation of the modern Christian is different from Christians of previous ages, while not altogether dissimilar. It is similar because since the dawn of Christianity other major religions have existed and flourished. It is different because today, more than ever before, Christians have both intellectual and experiential access to the religions of the world. For instance, monolingual Christians do not need Sanskrit to read and appreciate the *Vedas*, *Upanishads* and *Bhagavad Gita* – important Hindu sacred texts. Commentaries and translations are available thanks to the pioneering work of a number of gifted European orientalists in the eighteenth and nineteenth centuries, such as Sir William Jones (1746–94), H. T. Colebrooke (1765–1837), H. H. Wilson (1786–1860) and William Carey (1761–1836) from Britain; H. Ritter (1791–1896), U. Wagner (1774–1833) and F. M. Muller (1832–1900) from Germany; A. H. Anquetil-Duperron (1731–1805), the Abbe J. A. Dubois (1765–1848) and C. Lassen (1800–76) from France; and Indian Sanskritists such as R. M. Roy (1774–1833).[2] Missionaries were also instrumental in disseminating information and increasing understanding of other religions; even if sometimes their sole aim was conversion. Such was the purpose of the first British Baptist missionary–orientalist, William Carey.

If, in the West, knowledge of other religions increased in proportion to the development of scholarly sciences such as anthropology, sociology of religion, history of religions and oriental studies, as well as better communications and travel, the nineteenth and twentieth centuries witnessed further important developments.[3] Concerning the religiously plural society of North America, Robert Ellwood writes: 'Asian religion in North America falls into two categories: that imported by the large number of Chinese, Korean, Japanese, South East Asian and Indian immigrants who have come to American shores; and that oriented primarily to spiritual seekers of occidental background.'[4]

If Cook had set sail to discover foreign lands and initiate empire-building, the winds began to change course in the nineteenth and twentieth centuries, bringing waves of immigrants from East to West. Today, the skylines in most major cities in Europe, England and the United States are characterized not only by churches, but also Islamic mosques, Hindu temples, Sikh gurdwaras, Buddhist temples or meditation centres and, of course, Jewish synagogues – alongside a host of new religious movements and their architectural presence.

Ellwood pinpoints two factors: immigration and the new interest by young Americans in oriental religions. This latter factor reflects the decline of traditional Christianity in the West and the growing crisis in religious faith since the Enlightenment.[5] Cook's era had witnessed a strong, confident and often aggressive Christianity. Today, Christianity is reeling from internal theological crises as well as a missionary history inextricably tied up with colonialism. Furthermore, in some cases, the previously 'Establishment' religion of Christianity is now in competition with other religions. Daniel O'Hanlon, in his field studies on the background of Americans in Asia searching for spiritual sustenance, found 'that the majority were ex-Jews, ex-Catholics or ex-Protestants. The majority had found the religion of their early years empty rote and ritual . . . a few of them had found it heavy or oppressive'.[6] Harvey Cox, in his aptly named *Turning East* (1977), also traces the cause of this disillusionment with Christianity to the consumerism of American society. Cox's subtitle, *The Promise and the Peril of the New Orientalism*, brings us to the theological issues raised by this new situation.

THEOLOGICAL ISSUES

With the unavoidable consciousness that Christianity exists in a world of religious plurality, the Christian attitude to other religions is a pressing issue on today's theological agenda. The results of such theological reflection will affect a number of practical issues. For example: how should religious education be taught; what kind of social and political cooperation is permissible with people of other faiths; is it proper to use Buddhist meditational techniques for prayer or Hindu scriptures in the liturgy? On a less institutional level, those mixing daily with people from other religions are faced with more personally pressing questions: is the Hindu really damned because he or she is not a Christian? How can one appropriately maintain a Christian witness in a shared flat with three Sikh students? These questions, or at the very least their answers, will clearly be of interest to 'non-Christians'.[7]

For any honest Christian whose beliefs and life are integrated, these issues can only be resolved through theological reflection, social interaction and prayer. These questions are no longer the sole preserve of missionaries in exotic lands.

The central theological question tackled in this book is whether salvation is possible outside Christianity. In addressing this issue, I examine a host of related theological topics as well as tentatively answering the preceding practical questions. It will be clear that while I do not explicitly attend to the question of salvation within traditionally understood 'non-religious' movements, such as Marxism, Communism, Humanism and so on, I implicitly address this issue in dealing with the question of salvation *outside Christianity*. Very briefly, let us look at some of the questions ahead.

The difficulties can be conveniently focused in relation to two traditionally held Christian axioms. The first states that salvation is *through Jesus Christ alone*. If salvation is through Christ alone and there is no salvation outside Christianity (and Jesus did say according to John's gospel: 'I am the way, and the truth, and the life; no one comes to the Father, but by me', John 14:6), can the Christian still believe in a God who desires the salvation of all humankind (Acts 14:17; I Timothy 2:4; Romans 2:6–7)? Could a loving God consign the majority of humankind to perdition because these people did not know Jesus, often through no fault of their own? What also of the experience of 'holiness' which one may encounter in a Buddhist friend or within the Muslim religion? Are these experiences deceptive? Related to this, one may ask what form missionary activity should take? Furthermore, is there anything of worth to be learned from other religions, or are they properly characterized, as some Christians would argue, as sinful grasping after idols?

Alternatively, if the stress falls on the second axiom that *God desires the salvation of all humankind*, is this salvation gained *through* or *despite* the non-Christian religions? If, on the one hand, salvation occurs through these religions, is there any need for mission? And what of Jesus' claim that he alone is 'the way, and the truth, and the life' and Christianity's claim to absoluteness? What of those within certain religions who do not even believe in a god, such as the Theravadin Buddhist or Advaitin Hindu? And what exactly is the status and worth of non-Christian scriptures, practices and beliefs? Are they all of equal value and if not, by what criteria should one decide?

If, however, salvation can be found outside Christianity but only despite, and not through the various religions, then how precisely does this happen? Will it occur through death-bed confrontation, or special interior revelation, or perhaps a rational assent to God? But do these explanatory theories do justice to the social and historical nature of men and women and the communitarian character of religion? And what of those non-Christians who seem to reflect the 'presence of God' in their lives before they are on their death beds? Will the attendant understanding of the nature and purpose of mission therefore differ from those who believe that no salvation is possible outside Christianity? Within this perspective, what is the perceived value of non-Christian scriptures, practices and beliefs?

Clearly, a host of complicated and intriguing theological questions present themselves, with as much peril as promise! Both elements have determined the title of the final chapter of this book: Towards a Christian Theology of Religions. By a 'Christian' theology of religions, rather than a 'World' theology of religions or any other such phrase, I intend what Cornelius Ernst has expressed so succinctly: the

> activity of self-understanding . . . the explanatory, continually renewed effort within the Christian tradition to examine the implications of that tradition where it is continually being interrogated by the conjectures of historical change; the diversification of human experience by factors which are not themselves at the very least explicitly given in that tradition. The entrance of world religions into the course of European history forms one series of such factors of diversification.[8]

How should we proceed through this maze of difficulties that touch upon the perennial issues of the nature of God, the human person, Christ, the Christian Church and its mission, creation and history? In other words, what is the impact and challenge of the world religions upon Christology, ecclesiology and missiology?[9] I have chosen the following procedure to tackle the issues before us. Initially, I shall give a brief introduction to some of the varying Christian attitudes to other religions during the twentieth century. Admittedly, such an overview will be selective; however, I will indicate works in which more extensive surveys are found as I do not wish to duplicate easily accessible material. Furthermore, I have limited the scope of this purview to theological reflection in England, the United States, Europe and India and have only chosen certain major figures. This historical and bibliographical survey should help the reader make better use of the bibliography at the end of this book.[10] This panorama should also alert the reader to the complexity and nuances of the debate and give an impression of the emerging issues involved in formulating a Christian theology of religions.

Such a guide will also help to isolate the different paradigms underlying the various Christian attitudes. I use the term 'paradigm' in a sense analogous to that proposed by the philosopher of science, Thomas Kuhn – as a whole set of methods and procedures dictated by a central problem-solving model.[11] Practitioners within one paradigm tend to share a number of basic presuppositions dictating their attitudes and approaches to problem-solving. If our problem is the relation of Christianity to other religions, then the paradigmatic pre-suppositions will be certain theological tenets which dictate the approach towards an answer. Such a model also usefully accommodates diversity within a paradigm (we will see many nuances within a single type of approach) while facilitating inspection of the key issues determining each paradigm.

From this critical survey, my contention is that three dominant paradigms emerge from the recent history of theo-logical reflection, usefully providing a conceptual matrix within which the theological issues are highlighted. By then examin-ing a major representative of each of these three paradigmatic positions, in chapters 2–4, I will explore and analyse the theological issues in greater depth. Another advantage in so focusing the discussion is the implicit creation of a trialogue between the three representatives, thereby contrasting and comparing their positions while critically analysing their presuppositions, so that in my final chapter I will be able to develop a 'Christian theology of religions'.

TWENTIETH CENTURY CHRISTIAN ATTITUDES TO OTHER RELIGIONS

The background 1900–50

To set the scene I shall first consider Protestant (including ecumenical) and Roman Catholic (which I shall term Catholic) thought on this subject during the first half of the century.

Protestant and ecumenical theology　During this period much heated and creative discussion took place in missionary circles. Three distinctive paths through the landscape can be discerned. The Scottish Protestant missionary in India John Farquhar, in his *The Crown of Hinduism* (1913), gave forceful and clear expression to the view that Christ (and not Christianity) was the fulfilment and crown of Hinduism, analogous to Christ's fulfilment of the law and prophets of Judaism. Farquhar argued that this fulfilment applied to the theology, philosophy and practice of Hinduism. For him, missionary activity sought not to destroy but to fulfil the potential in Hinduism, which only Christ could bring to fruition.[12] Hence, in this view Hinduism is understood as included within the Christian plan of salvation. In Farquhar's words: 'Christ provides the fulfilment of each of the highest aspirations and aims of Hinduism . . . In Him is focused every ray of light that shines in Hinduism. He is the Crown of the Faith of India.'[13] This inclusivist note was echoed in later theology, especially in Roman Catholic circles, fulfilling Farquhar's position, with an emphasis on the fulfilment taking place through the Christian Church and not in Christ alone. I shall call this paradigmatic approach 'inclusivist'.

Another emerging attitude during this period is exemplified in the writings of the German liberal Protestant Ernst Troeltsch, in his essay, 'The Place of Christianity Among the World Religions' (1923), and in the American philosopher William Hocking's *Re-thinking Missions* (1932). Both were keenly aware of and emphasized historical and cultural relativism and argued that Christianity could not viably claim special status among the world religions, but should be seen as just one among many equally salvific paths to the divine reality. Their thought signalled a radical shift of emphasis away from both the missionary task of the Church in terms of preaching and evangelization, and the claim that the sole revelation of God was in Christ. Here the stress was upon a future of mutual enrichment and a transformation of Christianity and the other religions through their progressive interaction.

Troeltsch, for instance, acknowledged the manifestation and experiences of 'Divine Life' within Christianity through Christ, while significantly adding that this 'experience is undoubtedly the criterion of its validity, but, be it noted, only of its validity *for us*'.[14] Hocking argued that traditional mission required supplementation by a different form of institution reflecting this new attitude. In a later book he wrote:

> The mission is set for teaching; the required institution must be set for learning as well. The mission is set for announcement of doctrine; this institution must be set as well for conversation and conference . . . The mission is set for address to its own region; this institution must be set for give and take with the thought and feeling of a nation and a world.[15]

Hocking went so far as to suggest the future emergence of a world faith. As the various religions reconceived themselves in the light of truths from other religions, they would slowly recognize a common essence and would one day eventually unite together in a world faith, rid of their irreconcilable differences. Nevertheless, Hocking thought that the world religions would and should retain their different identities: 'In proportion as any religion grows in self-understanding through grasping its own essence, it grasps the essence of all religion, and gains in power to interpret its various forms.'[16]

The views of Troeltsch and Hocking encouraged and validated religious pluralism. I shall call this kind of approach 'pluralist'.

However, Hendrik Kraemer, a Dutch missionary deeply influenced by the German Protestant theologians Karl Barth and Emil Brunner, forcefully challenged both Farquhar and Hocking. In his very influential and controversial works, especially *The Christian Message in a Non-Christian World* (1938) and *Religion and the Christian Faith* (1956), Kraemer propounded a dialectical theology which stressed Christ's relationship to the religions as one of discontinuity and judgement, rather than fulfilment (Farquhar) and mutual appreciation (Hocking). Although Kraemer was not uncritical of Christianity as a religion, he thought that its special relationship to Christ gave it unique status among the world religions. Kraemer sharply criticized the reduction of evangelism to social service and mutual enrichment. He also insisted that conversion to Christ and his cross could not be minimized in the Christian encounter with other faiths. The missionary's sole aim was 'to persuade the non-Christian world to surrender to Christ as the sole Lord of Life'.[17] Kraemer has been rightly

evaluated as the 'major spokesman and representative' of the 'exclusivist school'.[18]

This approach then, which I shall call 'exclusivist', characterized the three great International Missionary Conferences held at Edinburgh (1910), Jerusalem (1928) and Tambaram (1938).[19] This approach also dominated the World Council of Churches under the Directorship of Willem Visser't Hooft until his retirement in 1966. Visser't Hooft wrote that 'the attitude of the Christian Church to the religions can ... only be the attitude of the witness who points to the one Lord Jesus Christ as Lord of all men'.[20]

Variations of these three paradigms (inclusivist, pluralist and exclusivist) characterize the discussion that has continued during the latter half of the century.[21]

Roman Catholic theology The majority of Catholic theologians concerned with these questions in this period were European scholastics. Consequently, much of the discussion on the salvation of non-Christians (technically designated 'infidels') followed Thomist lines. Philippe Glorieux developed Thomas Aquinas's early remarks that God would 'reveal by internal inspiration what [the good infidel following the dictates of their conscience] has to believe'.[22] Glorieux argued that a special death-bed illumination would be granted to the good infidel, thereby allowing an assent of faith necessary for salvation.[23] Ricardo Lombardi followed the later thought of Aquinas, which stressed the assent to God by means of natural reason: 'When a man arrives [morally] at the age of reason, the first thing to which his mind must turn is to deliberate about himself. And if he directs himself towards the true end, grace is given to him and original sin is remitted.'[24]

Lombardi, in *The Salvation of the Unbeliever* (1956), also developed Aquinas's argument that this rational assent contained an implicit desire for baptism into the Church. His book contains a useful analysis of earlier theories; one such, worth mentioning, was Cardinal Billot's theory. Disturbed by his French contemporaries' inability to arrive at theism through the use of reason, Billot argued that infidels possessed the moral level of infants, thereby declaring them morally inculpable and destined to limbo, as were infants.[25]

These scholars laboured under the often rigidly interpreted

Catholic axiom, *extra ecclesiam nulla salus* (no salvation outside the Church), solemnly promulgated at the Council of Florence (1438–45).[26] The difference between the Catholic axiom and Kraemer's position was the Catholic stress on the Church, rather than Kraemer's Protestant stress on Christ alone.[27]

However, a group of mainly French and Belgian Catholics in India propounded a form of inclusivist theology in the light of their studies of, and encounters with, the Hindu tradition of Advaita Vedanta. In 1950 the French orientalist Jules Monchanin, and his Benedictine monk friend Henri le Saux (later called Swami Abhishiktananda), founded an Indian-Christian ashram on the banks of the Kavery River at Kulitalai in Tamil Nadu, South India. The ashram was pertinently named *Saccidananda*, after the Hindu characterization of divine reality, interpreted as *Sat* (Being), *Cit* (Logos – the Word), *Ananda* (Bliss of Love and Beauty). There they meshed together Hindu spirituality and a Benedictine monasticism to forge what they perceived as a totally Indian, totally Christian lifestyle. This included using the *Vedas* for meditative readings and chanting Sanskrit prayers in the liturgy. In 1951 they wrote of this experiment in *An Indian Benedictine Ashram*.[28] Monchanin thought that: 'Advaita (non-dualism) and the praise of the Trinity are our only aim. This means that we must grasp the authentic Hindu search for God in order to Christianize it, starting with ourselves first of all, from within.'[29]

The motivation for their work was clearly inclusivist ('we must grasp the authentic Hindu search for God in *order to Christianize it*'), although their ashram would no doubt have been encouraged by pluralists such as Hocking.[30]

In 1922, 17 years before Monchanin arrived in India, two Belgian Jesuits, Pierre Johanns and George Dandoy founded a journal, *The Light of the East* (vols 1–12, 1922–34), in which they stated that they wished to 'help India ... to know and understand Jesus ... We have no intention to put out the existing lights. Rather we shall try to show that the best thought of the east is a bud that fully expanded blossoms into Christian thought.'[31]

Catholic thought had itself to await full blossoming until after the mid 1960s, with the advent of the Second Vatican Council's proclamation on the non-Christian religions. The teachings set forth by such Councils have authoritative status for Roman Catholics. The inclusivists mentioned above represent exceptions to the otherwise prevailing exclusivist attitudes within Catholicism.[32]

The foreground: 1950 to the present day

After two world wars, the disintegration of empires and the upsurge of new theological currents, the three main paths I have outlined traversed varying contours in the changing historical and theological terrain. It was increasingly felt that mission must be separated from religious imperialism, while social service and proclamation came to be seen as inseparably connected.[33] The understanding of the Church took on a sacramental and social, rather than institutional, character especially in Roman Catholic circles. Furthermore, many Christians had become deeply impressed by various religions and less confident about their own previous claims.

Protestant and ecumenical theology   In the late 1960s, under the direction of the Indian Christian Stanley Samartha, the World Council of Churches Department of Dialogue with People of Living Faiths and Ideologies forged a path between a weakened form of inclusivist theology and a strong version of pluralist practice. Two consultations edited by Samartha reflect this new mood: *Living Faiths and Ultimate Goals* (1974) and *Towards World Community: Resources and Responsibilities for Living Together* (1975). The first title indicates the strong respect, without compromise on beliefs in ultimate goals, towards the lives and beliefs of people from other faiths. Marxism, also considered a living faith, was represented in the first consultation. The second title stresses the urgency of the social tasks which now preoccupied mission thinking. Samartha's views reflect this variation of inclusivism. He affirms the decisive, but not exclusively unique, revelation of God in Christ. He also reports that the fulfilment approach is often 'regarded as patronizing by our neighbors' whose religions he sees as 'alternative ways of salvation'.[34] Samartha characteristically adds that demanding acceptance of Christ prior to 'sharing with our neighbors the love of God . . . is unhelpful'.[35]

Among Protestant theologians inclusivism is becoming

popular. However, this tendency is increasingly marked by a reticence towards any evangelical form of mission demanded by exclusivists such as Kraemer, and a tacit theological encouragement of religious pluralism. One reason for this is reflected in the title of the late English Anglican bishop John Robinson's book, *Truth is Two-Eyed* (1979). Rather than stress the fulfilment of Hinduism in its encounter with Christ, Robinson argued that Christianity itself is fulfilled in its encounter with Hinduism![36] Robinson showed that Christian myopic vision is enriched and fulfilled in the light of Hindu reflections on the personal and material world. Two eyes on the truth are better than one, although the focus for both lenses, so to speak, is Christ. Like Samartha, he holds to the definitiveness of the revelation of God in Christ, without denying that God has revealed Himself elsewhere: 'To believe that God is best defined by Christ is not to believe that God is confined to Christ.'[37]

Earlier, across the Atlantic, this same thrust was apparent in Paul Tillich's stimulating attempt to mediate between the pluralism of Troeltsch and the exclusivism of Barth and Kraemer. Starting from a somewhat different approach to Robinson, Tillich acknowledges the experience of the holy in all religions and affirms, like Robinson, that the crucified Jesus is the most valuable criterion for discerning God's activity within the history of religions. Robinson said that in the criterion of Jesus 'as embodying, fleshing out, the saving disclosure and act of God', one holds 'the conviction, always to be clarified, completed and corrected in dialogue, that it is this [criterion] which offers the profoundest clue to all the rest.'[38] Tillich writes that in the image of the crucified Christ: 'the criteria are given under which Christianity must judge itself and, by judging itself, judge also the other religions and the quasi-religions'.[39]

Tillich and Robinson pay little attention to the implications for mission and ecclesiology, but their Christological criterion for evaluating other religions places them firmly in the inclusivist–fulfilment category. Tillich's words characterize this weaker form of inclusivism: 'Not conversion, but dialogue. It would be a tremendous step forward if Christianity were to accept this.'[40]

Another American implicitly within this tradition is the process theologian–philosopher John Cobb. His book, *Beyond Dialogue: Towards a Mutual Transformation of Christianity and Buddhism* (1982), offers a vision of transformation that is similar to Hocking's, without the assumption of a common future essence. His thrust is akin to Robinson's, although he goes as far as to suggest to Buddhists certain transformations that could occur within their own tradition, such as the idea that 'Amida is Christ' – or expressive of the 'Logos which Christians know as incarnate in Jesus.'[41] Cobb represents a somewhat abstract process form of inclusivism.

In Europe, Tillich's work has been a source of stimulation for the German Lutheran Wolfhart Pannenberg. Stressing the importance of the history of religions, combined with his own eschatological[42] perspective, Pannenberg remains within the inclusivist tradition:

> The history of religions even beyond the time of the public ministry of Jesus, presents itself as the history of the appearances of the God who revealed himself through Jesus.[43]

Another German Lutheran, Jurgen Moltmann, like Hendrik Kraemer, strongly relativizes the Church and Christianity. This reflects his Barthian heritage. However, fulfilment for him is not in terms of the Church or Christ explicitly, but in the creation of hope. He writes that the main aim of mission should be to '"infect" people, whatever their religion, with the spirit of hope, love and responsibility for the world'.[44] But, for Moltmann, Christ is the original source of all hope, love and responsibility: 'Outside Christ no salvation. Christ has come and was sacrificed for the reconciliation of the whole world. No one is excluded.'[45]

This multi-faceted inclusivist development has come under fire from opposite theological wings, often repeating, but also furthering, the discussion that took place in the first half of the century.

Pluralists, developing the impetus of Troeltsch and Hocking, argue that Christ's decisiveness should be understood as a personal confession without objective or universally binding status. This follows Troeltsch's 'only ... for us' emphasis. Consequently, many pluralists argue that Christians should not evaluate other religions through Christological spectacles but must re-think issues in the light of the data from all the religions, developing a sort of world theology. A major proponent of this view is the English Presbyterian philosopher of religion and theologian, John Hick. His theology of religions and criticisms of Christology, ecclesiology and missiology can be found initially in *God and the Universe of Faiths*, first published in 1973, and more recently in *God has Many Names* (1980, US ed. 1982). Hick places much emphasis upon the universal salvific will of God: 'Can we then accept the conclusion that the God of love who seeks to save all mankind has nevertheless ordained that men must be saved in such a way that only a small minority can in fact receive this salvation?'[46] Hick's answer is 'No!' He has also developed a global theology of the after-life with references to Christian, Hindu, Humanist and Buddhist sources in *Death and Eternal Life* (1976).

The historically, but less theologically, minded Canadian scholar Wilfred Cantwell Smith tackles the problem from a different angle. In *The Meaning and End of Religion*, first published in 1963, Smith attacks the very notion of 'religion' as an abstract and unhelpful reification, encouraging 'us–them' thinking. He also argues for a common religious unity in 'faith' as distinguished from the various 'cumulative traditions' – the historical accumulation of creeds, liturgies and institutions. He further reflects on the task of developing a global theology in the light of this common core of faith in *Towards a World Theology* (1980). The English historian Arnold Toynbee, in his *Christianity Among the Religions of the World* (1957) also follows Troeltsch's pluralism, as does the Anglican theologian Alan Race in his *Christians and Religious Pluralism* (1983).

In part, these works represent the liberal reaction against harsh versions of exclusivist theology, such as propounded at the Congress on World Mission at Chicago in 1960. The Congress announced: 'In the years since the war, more than one billion souls have passed into eternity and more than half of these went to the torment of hell fire without even hearing of Jesus Christ, who He was, or why He died on the cross of Calvary.'[47]

More recently, the 'Frankfurt Declaration' (1970), composed by mainly German Lutherans who felt dissatisfied with the approach of the World Council and other Christian bodies, clearly refuted any idea of fulfilment or compromise on mission: 'We refute the idea that 'Christian presence' among the adherents to the world religions and a give-and-take dialogue with them are substitutes for a proclamation of the Gospel which aims at conversion. Such dialogues simply establish good points of contact for missionary communication.'[48]

For both Hick and Smith, like the previous group of inclusivists, there is an acceptance of religious plurality. But Hick and Smith add a positive and explicit encouragement of, and theological justification for, religious pluralism. They stress, like Hocking and Troeltsch their predecessors, the learning and growth that takes place through encounter. While both tend to neglect ecclesiological questions, Hick had dwelt upon the related Christological issues. These modern day pluralists have sometimes been criticized for their allegedly vague and obscure understanding of God and their relativizing of religious truth.

Equally opposed to the various inclusivist approaches and the developed pluralism of Hick and Smith are neo-Kraemerians such as the late bishop of the Church of South India, Stephen Neill (*Christian Faith and Other Faiths*, 1970, revised as *Crises in Belief*, 1984), bishop Lesslie Newbigin (in *The Open Secret*, 1978), and the English lawyer, Islamicist and evangelical, Norman Anderson (in *Christianity and Comparative Religion*, 1971). While Neill, Newbigin and Anderson acknowledge that God operates outside ecclesiological Christianity, Anderson characteristically denies that 'other religions' may be viewed as 'saving structures'.[49] These exclusivists, although not uncritical of Kraemer, emphasize the proclamation of the Word. However, they also stress a social involvement with, and a deep appreciation of, other faiths and cultures. They maintain that the Gospel is compromised in the inclusivist and pluralist approaches, and that ecclesiology, missiology and Christology are thereby neglected.

Nuances within the exclusivist approach are evident. These modern exclusivists have been criticized as to the authority of their biblical foundations, their minimizing of revelation outside Christianity and even, in some cases, their triumphalism and racism.[50]

Roman Catholic theology After the relatively quiet period before Vatican II's important *Declaration on the Relation of the Church to Non-Christian Religions* (1965), Roman Catholic theology blossomed, or even erupted, into fruitful discussion.

The debate mainly moved along the fulfilment and exclusivist paths, with a tendency to view pluralism as a species of indifferentism.

A major figure, whose influence dominates Catholic debate, is the late German Jesuit Karl Rahner. His main writings on this topic are found in his *Theological Investigations*, published in twenty volumes between 1961 and 1984. In these works Rahner coined the term 'anonymous Christian'. This term refers to a non-Christian who gains salvation through faith, hope and love by the grace of Christ, mediated however imperfectly through his or her own religion, which thereby points towards its historical fulfilment in Christ and his Church. For Rahner, grace, Christology and ecclesiology are inseparable. He tries to hold two axioms together: 'God desires the salvation of every-one. And this salvation willed by God is the salvation won by Christ'.[51] In this way many Catholic theologians are able to interpret the 'no salvation outside the Church' axiom, aided by a more sacramental understanding of the Church initiated by Vatican II.

If Robinson and Tillich represent the liberal wing of inclusiv-ism, Rahner, while firmly planted within the same tradition, occupies a more conservative position. While Robinson and Tillich emphasize Christ alone, Rahner emphasizes both Christ and his Church.

The Catholic discussion may be profitably charted in relation to Rahner's version of inclusivism. On the one hand, exclusivist theologians attacked Rahner for minimizing mission, dissolv-ing the character of the Church and Christian discipleship, and compromising the cross and proclamation of Christ. Such were the criticisms of the Dutch Jesuit missionary Henricus van Straelen in *The Catholic Encounter with World Religions* (1966), the Swiss theologian Hans von Balthasar in *The Moment of Christian Witness* (1969), and the German oriental-ist convert to Catholicism Paul Hacker in *Theological Found-ations of Evangelization* (1980). On the other hand, liberal Catholics like the Swiss Hans Küng joined pluralists like Hick in criticizing Rahner's ecclesiocentricism.[52] However, Küng is himself criticized by Hick for his Christocentricism.[53] Küng allows other religions a provisional but genuine salvific value, but then suggests an 'existential confrontation' with Christ after death, echoing Glorieux's theory.[54] The missionary

Eugene Hillman criticizes Rahner's suggestion that Christians have a better chance of salvation, but agrees with the notion of the 'anonymous Christian'. In *The Wider Ecumenism: Anonymous Christianity and the Church* (1968), Hillman discusses further important contributions by Catholic theologians such as Edward Schillebeeckx, Heinz Schlette, Yves Congar and Henri de Lubac. Küng, Hillman and the authors cited above may all be classed as inclusivists. Variations within this tradition are clearly evident.

However, a small number of influential American Catholics have adopted a Hickian form of pluralism, criticizing even liberal inclusivists like Küng. Paul Knitter's *No Other Name? A Critical Survey of Christian Attitudes towards the World Religions* (1985) (which also contains a magisterial survey of different responses to religious pluralism) exemplifies this position, as do the writings of Rosemary Ruether and Gregory Baum.[55]

Catholics in India, as before, have been especially creative. Klaus Klostermaier's stimulating and vivid book *Hindu and Christian in Vrindaban* (1969) is critical of pronouncements from European armchair theologians, and in *Kristvidya* (1967) he gives expression to an Indian Christology in terms of the Hindu thought world. Klostermaier follows in the tradition of Monchanin. Also in this tradition, Rayumando Panikkar had fused together fulfilment theology and the urgency for an enriching indigenous theology in his classic book, *The Unknown Christ of Hinduism* (1964, revised edition 1981). In *The Trinity and the Religious Experience of Man* (1973), he further argues that the three aspects of the Trinity provide a useful framework for understanding religious plurality – truth can even be three-eyed! His massive *Myth, Faith and Hermeneutics* (1979) is an illuminating exegesis of Hindu mythology in a similar vein to Robinson and Cobb, but far surpassing their work in erudition and orientalist skills.

Following Panikkar, although less conceptual and more concerned with spirituality, is Abhishiktananda's successor at Saccidananda Ashram, the Englishman Bede Griffiths. His most important works are *Return to the Centre* (1978) and *The Marriage of East and West* (1982). Sister Vandana's *Social Justice and Ashrams* (1982) seeks to relate the spirituality of the ashram movement to social service – a theme often stressed in Indian Catholic circles.[56]

My observations have concentrated upon individual theologians. An excellent study of more institutional developments reflecting Christian attitudes to other religions can be found in Marcus Braybrooke's *Inter-Faith Organizations, 1893–1979: A Historical Directory* (1980) and Walbert Buhlmann's journalistic *All Have the Same God* (1979).

CONCLUSION

In this brief survey I have tried to isolate the dominant paradigms underlying the different Christian attitudes to other religions – pluralism, exclusivism and inclusivism. I have also tried to highlight some of the issues concerning Christ, the Church, and the nature of mission as well as the variety of emphases within each paradigm. It appears that two underlying theological axioms are implicitly determinative of the various paradigms: *the universal salvific will of God* and the claim that it is *only in Christ (or his Church) that men and women can be saved*. The three paradigmatic positions, I will contend, are generated from an emphasis on either one or both of these axioms.

It can be argued, and I shall do so presently, that the best representatives of the three positions who have also written extensively in English (or in English translation) are John Hick (pluralism), Hendrik Kraemer (exclusivism) and Karl Rahner (inclusivism). I now intend to study these three theologians in detail to pursue the complex theological issues posed by the challenge of other religions.

NOTES

1. D. Pailin, *Attitudes to Other Religions: Comparative Religion in Seventeenth and Eighteenth Century Britain* (1984).
2. See, for instance, J. R. Rayapati, *Early American Interest in Vedanta* (1973) for the influence of orientalist translations on early American thought. For the orientalist influence on Hinduism, see D. Kopf, *British Orientalism and the Bengal Renaissance* (1969). For orientalism in Europe, see P. Hacker, 'Schopenhauer

und die Ethik des Hinduismus' in *Kleine Schriften* (1978), pp. 531–65.

3. E. Sharpe, *Comparative Religion: a History* (1975) charts the influence of these various disciplines from the nineteenth century onwards.

4. R. Ellwood, 'Asian religions in North America', *Concilium* 161 (1983), p. 17, and his *Alternative Altars: Unconventional and Eastern Spirituality in America* (1979).

5. For a historical survey of the impact of the Enlightenment, see G. Cragg, *The Church and the Age of Reason 1648–1798* (1983).

6. D. O'Hanlon, 'A view of the US scene from Asia through American eyes', *Concilium*, 161 (1983), p. 34.

7. Throughout this book the expression 'non-Christian' is used not pejoratively, but simply to designate, within a single umbrella term, the variety of different beliefs and ways of life other than the Christian.

8. C. Ernst, *Multiple Echo* (1979), p. 30.

9. These terms are used throughout the book with the following meanings. 'Christology' relates to questions concerning the nature and person of Christ – for example, was he divine, and if so, in what way can one coherently speak of this divinity? 'Ecclesiology' refers to questions concerning the nature and purpose of the Christian Church – for example, what is the relation of the Church to the person of Christ? 'Missiology' refers to questions concerning the scope, intentions and methods of proclaiming the Gospel – for example, how should, if at all, the Gospel be proclaimed to Jewish people?

10. See also my forthcoming book, *Christianity and the Encounter with Other Religions: A Bibliographical Guide* (1987).

11. T. Kuhn, *The Structure of Scientific Revolutions* (1970).

12. For examples of other like-minded theologians of this period and a further discussion of Farquhar, see E. Sharpe, *Not to Destroy but to Fulfil* (1965).

13. J. Farquhar, *The Crown of Hinduism* (1913), pp. 457–8. E. Dewick, like many others, notes that this approach 'can be traced, almost (though perhaps not quite) continuously throughout the history of the Church': *The Christian Attitude to Other Religions* (1953), p. 120.

14. E. Troeltsch, 'The Place of Christianity Among the World Religions' in *Christian Thought: Its History and Application* (1957), p. 26.

15. W. Hocking, *Living Religions and a World Faith* (1940), p. 205.

16. Ibid., p. 198.

17. H. Kraemer, *The Christian Message in a Non-Christian World* (1938), p. 444.

18. A. Camps, *Partners in Dialogue: Christianity and the Other World Religions* (1983), p. 22.

19. On the complex background to these conferences, see C. Hallencreutz, *From Kraemer Towards Tambaram: A Study in Hendrik Kraemer's Missionary Approach* (1966), and W. R. Hogg, *Ecumenical Foundations: A History of the International Missionary Council and its Nineteenth Century Background* (1952).

20. W. Visser't Hooft, *No Other Name: The Choice between Syncretism and Universalism* (1963), p. 116.

21. Good theological and historical surveys of this period, not already mentioned, are E. O. Jathanna, *The Decisiveness of the Christ-Event* (1981); C. Hallencreutz, *New Approaches to Men of Other Faiths, 1938–1968: A Theological Discussion* (1970); M. Warren's study of the social, economic and religious factors in mission history, *Social History and Christian Mission* (1967); and S. Neill, *A History of the Church: Christian Missions* (1964), esp. chs 10–13 and the extensive bibliography.

22. Thomas Aquinas, *De Veritate Catholicae Fidei* 14, 11.

23. P. Glorieux, 'Endurcissement final et graces dernieres', *Nouvelle Revue Theologique*, 59 (1932), pp. 865–92, and 'De la necessite des missions ou du probleme du salut infideles', *Union Missionaraire*, Supplement, January 1933.

24. Thomas Aquinas, *Summa Theologiae*, I–II, q.89, a.6.

25. L. Billot, 'La Providence divine et le nombre infini d'hommes hors de la voie normale du salut', *Etudes*, nine articles in vols 161–76, 1919–23.

26. H. Denzinger, *The Sources of Catholic Dogma* (1957), p. 714.

27. M. Eminyan, *The Theology of Salvation* (1960), contains a scholarly survey and comprehensive bibliography of European Catholic theology in this period.

28. Abhishiktananda and J. Monchanin, *An Indian Benedictine Ashram* (1951). The revised edition is entitled *A Benedictine Ashram* (1964).

29. Quoted in J. Weber (ed.), *In Quest of the Absolute: The Life and Works of Jules Monchanin* (1977), p. 6.

30. See Hocking, *Living Religions*, pp. 206ff, where he recognizes the special potential of the Roman Catholic missions.

31. *Light of the East*, 1 (1922), pp. 1–2.

32. A lucid survey of Catholic attitudes, to Hinduism in particular, during this era can be found in J. Mattam's *Land of the Trinity: A Study of Modern Christian Approaches to Hinduism* (1975), which also contains an extensive bibliography.

33. In *Evangelism in Eclipse* (1979), H. Hoekstra argues that the notion of evangelical mission in the World Council of Churches has become largely eclipsed by a one-sided stress on social and political

liberation. For Hoekstra, the pendulum has swung too far.

34. G. Anderson and T. Stransky (eds), *Christ's Lordship and Religious Pluralism* (1981), pp. 35–6.
35. Ibid., p. 55.
36. A. Camps, the Dutch Catholic missiologist, charts the impact of various religions on Christian communities in different parts of the world in his *Partners in Dialogue.*
37. J. A. T. Robinson, *Truth is Two-Eyed* (1979), p. 129.
38. Ibid., pp. 119, 129.
39. P. Tillich, *Christianity and the Encounter of the World Religions* (1963), p. 82.
40. Ibid., p. 95.
41. J. Cobb, *Beyond Dialogue: Towards a Mutual Transformation of Christianity and Buddhism* (1982), pp. 123–8.
42. 'Eschatology' relates to teachings about events at the end of time.
43. W. Pannenberg, *Basic Questions in Theology*, vol. 2 (1971), p. 115.
44. J. Moltmann, *The Church in the Power of the Spirit* (1977), p. 152.
45. Ibid., p. 153.
46. J. Hick, *God and the Universe of Faiths* (1977).
47. J. Percy (ed.), *Facing the Unfinished Task: Messages Delivered at the Congress on World Mission* (1961), p. 9.
48. The full text of the Declaration is in *Christianity Today*, 14 (1970), pp. 844–6.
49. J. N. Anderson (ed.), *The World Religions* (1975), p. 236. See also bishop G. Lindbeck's exclusivist approach from a socio-linguistic perspective: *The Nature of Doctrine: Religion and Theology in a Postliberal Age* (1984), ch. 3.
50. Anderson and Stransky (eds), *Christ's Lordship*, p. 76.
51. K. Rahner, *Theological Investigations*, vol. 5 (1966), p. 122.
52. H. Kung, *On Being a Christian* (1976), pp. 97–8.
53. Hick, *Universe of Faiths*, pp. 128ff.
54. J. Neuner (ed.), *Christian Revelation and World Religions* (1967), p. 52.
55. R. Reuther, 'An invitation to Jewish–Christian dialogue. In what sense can we say that Jesus was the "Christ"?', *The Ecumenist*, 10 (1972), pp. 17–24; G. Baum, 'Christianity and other religions: a Catholic problem', *Cross Currents* 16 (1966).
56. The many sides of the Catholic debate were well expressed in an American symposium, L. Rouner (ed.), *Religious Pluralism* (1984), and especially at the Nagpur Theological Conference in 1971, M. Dhavamony (ed.), *Evangelism, Dialogue and Development* (1972).

CHAPTER 2

The Pluralist Paradigm

The pluralist paradigm has been characterized as one that maintains that other religions are equally salvific paths to the one God, and Christianity's claim that it is the only path (exclusivism), or the fulfilment of other paths (inclusivism), should be rejected for good theological and phenomenological reasons.

This position can be traced from Troeltsch and Hocking onwards and, although a minority view, it is gaining support in many quarters, both Protestant and Catholic.[1] Although this view has a number of able exponents, not without their differences, John Hick is arguably the most thorough and far-reaching representative. Paul Knitter correctly judges that 'Hick is the most radical, the best-known, and therefore the most controversial of the proponents of a theocentric model for Christian approaches to other religions.'[2] Hick has also stimulated pluralist thinkers within other religions.[3]

As a main representative of pluralism, I shall examine Hick's thought in some detail, while also indicating the similarities and differences between him and other pluralists.[4] Through this case study it will become clear that many, though not all, of the comments on Hick's arguments and assumptions may be equally applied to his pluralist allies. By choosing a single representative rather than carrying out an extensive survey, I hope to focus upon and discuss pertinent theological and phenomenological issues central to the pluralist paradigm.

HICK'S REVOLUTION IN THE THEOLOGY OF RELIGIONS

John Harwood Hick was born in Scarborough, Yorkshire, on 20 January 1922. After an early conversion to 'a strong evangelical and indeed fundamentalist' type of Christianity, he became dissatisfied with his fellow evangelicals' 'narrowness and . . . lack of sympathy with questioning thought'.[5] After studying philosophy and theology at Edinburgh, Oxford and Cambridge, he lectured in the philosophy of religion in the United States and England before taking up the H. G. Wood Professorial Chair in Birmingham University's Theology Department in 1967. In multi-faith, multi-cultural Birmingham, Hick began to reflect on the relation of Christianity to other religions and underwent a further conversion – to a pluralist theology of religions.[6]

The publication of *God and the Universe of Faiths* in 1973 marked Hick's adoption of pluralism. Important to Hick's argument is his use of an astronomical analogy. Ptolemaic astronomers saw the earth at the centre of the universe and explained the movement of planets (which did not conform to the theory) by postulating 'epicycles'. The growing number of epicycles rendered the Ptolemaic view less and less plausible. Finally, the Copernican view in its simple explanation of the facts by the theory that the sun, rather than the earth, was at the centre of the universe, replaced the Ptolemaic cosmology. In an analogous manner, Hick thinks that the old Ptolemaic theology (represented by Kraemer and others) and its recent epicycles (represented by Rahner and others), prop up an increasingly implausible system with the Church/Christianity/ Christ at the centre of the universe of faiths. Consequently, he proposes a Copernican revolution in theology whereby Christians 'shift from the dogma that Christianity is at the centre to the realisation that it is *God* who is at the centre, and that all religions . . . including our own, serve and revolve around him.'[7]

Hick has constantly refined and developed this pluralist approach in the light of various criticisms. In 1982, he moved from one multi-faith environment to another, when he took up the Danforth Chair in the Philosophy of Religion at the Claremont Graduate School, California.

The theological arguments for Hick's Copernican revolution

Why did Hick demand a Copernican revolution in the Christian attitude to other religions? He characterized as 'Ptolemaic' the long-standing and dominant exclusivist view, both Catholic and Protestant, 'that outside the church, or outside Christianity, there is no salvation.'[8] This stance seemed blatantly incompatible with the venerable Christian axiom of God's universal salvific love and desire to save all people. Hick classifies Hendrik Kraemer as one who holds such a Ptolemaic position.

Hick also found fault with inclusivist developments. Of the many inclusivist theologies, he acknowledges that the 'best known attempt is that of Karl Rahner, with his concept of the anonymous Christian'.[9]

Although Rahner's position avoids consigning the majority of humankind to perdition, it is for Hick, 'too manifestly an ad hoc contrivance to satisfy many'.[10] For a start, it still implicitly holds to the exclusivist axiom, assuming 'without question that salvation is only in Christ and through incorporation into his mystical body, the church.'[11] For this reason, Hick calls these inclusivist developments Ptolemaic 'epicycles'. They attempt to accommodate new situations (with difficulty) without modifying their basic presuppositions. Furthermore, Hick argues that trusting and credible dialogue is manifestly unsatisfactory when a partner is designated an 'honorary Christian – and this even though they do not so regard themselves and even though they may insist that they are not Christians but Muslims, Jews, Hindus etc.'[12] This ploy can also be reversed and unfruitfully perpetuated, so that a Vedantin Hindu can call a Christian 'an "anonymous" Vedantist'.[13] 'Dialogue' on this premise is triumphalist and arrogant and will inevitably lead to a stalemate. In sum, this Ptolemaic development lacks credibility: 'When salvation is acknowledged to be taking place without any connection with the Christian Church or Gospel, in people who are living on the basis of quite other faiths, is it not a somewhat empty gesture to insist upon affixing a Christian label to them?'[14] Hence, according to Hick, the Ptolemaic position and its epicycles are untenable and should be abandoned.

Hick's primary theological argument for his Copernican theocentric revolution, away from an ecclesiocentric or Christocentric approach, is based on the affirmation of the *universal salvific will of God*: 'We say as Christians that God is the God of universal love, that he is the Creator and Father of all mankind, that he wills the ultimate good and salvation of all men.'[15] Hick asks whether such a God could have 'ordained that men must be saved in such a way that only a small minority can in fact receive this salvation?'[16] His answer is 'No'. It is precisely the doctrine of a God of universal love which dictates Hick's answer, and leads to a Copernican revolution in Christian theology. The theological axiom of the universal salvific will of God is a fundamental tenet of the pluralist paradigm.[17]

But what of the other major axiom, so determinative for Ptolemaic theologians and so central to the Christian tradition: that *salvation is found only through the grace of God in Christ*? Hick has been criticized for abandoning the central Christian truth of the incarnation and subverting the distinctiveness of Christianity.[18]

Hick argues that the problem with 'traditional' Christology lies in the literal understanding of the incarnation, which inevitably entails the unacceptable '*extra ecclesiam nulla salus*' doctrine:

> There is a direct line of logical entailment from the premise that Jesus was God ... to the conclusion that Christianity, and Christianity alone, was founded by God in person; and from all this to the conclusion that God must want all his human children to be related to him through this religion which he has himself founded for us.[19]

This unacceptable conclusion is only avoided if we work 'back up the chain of inference and eventually ... question the original premise' – that is 'traditional' Christology.[20] However, it should be noted that Hick's Christological reflections are not entirely determined by the problems of religious pluralism. Other religions, modern biblical scholarship and philosophical difficulties have cumulatively led to Hick's criticism of traditional Christology and his suggestion that the incarnation should be understood mythologically rather than literally. According to Hick, this understanding will also help to break the exclusivist chain of inference. I will briefly outline each of these areas in turn.

Other religions   Beside the unacceptable exclusivist implications of traditional Christology, Hick argues that there is a *natural religious tendency* to exalt a human founder to an elevated divine status, exemplified in, for example, the Mahayana Buddhist doctrine of the Three Bodies (*Trikaya*).[21] This strong and understandable tendency to transpose psychologically powerful and compelling experiences into universally binding and normative truths is exemplified in the language of a lover, who may say that his 'Helen is the sweetest girl in the world'.[22] Clearly, the lover's language properly expresses a personal and practical commitment to his Helen, rather than a historical-truth claim that if one searched the world no sweeter girl than Helen could be found. Hick suggests that we should view the language of religious commitment in a similar manner. The claim that Jesus is God incarnate expresses the religious significance and importance of Jesus to Christians, nothing more and nothing less.

Philosophical difficulties   Hick also approaches the question of Christology from another perspective. He investigates the logical status and nature of incarnational language. He employs a distinction between literal language and mythical or poetical language.[23] He further argues that truth may be predicated of myth, although it is a 'kind of practical truth' as opposed to a theoretical or literal truth.[24] For example:

> I may say of a certain happening that it is the work of the devil. If this is not literally true, the statement is mythic in character, and it is a true statement in so far as the attitude which it tends to evoke is appropriate to the actual character of the event in question.[25]

For Hick, when mythic language is confused with literal language, a false type of truth–claim is made. When, for instance, the mythic character of incarnational language is interpreted literally, the false chain-reaction leading to the exclusivist claim is set in action. In the analogous case of the lover and his Helen, this confusion results in a dubious historical claim about Helen's sweetness. Properly understood, incarnational language expresses and invokes for Christians the appropriate response to Jesus as saviour: 'For it is through Jesus that we have encountered God as our heavenly Father and have entered into a new life which has its ultimate centre in God.'[26] In sum, Hick argues that incarnational language is mythic and not literal in character. Such mythic language need not imply an exclusive revelation of God.

Hick raises one other philosophical difficulty with traditional Christology. He argues that the incarnation, literally understood, impossibly reconciles irreconcilables: '. . . how one person can be both eternal and yet born in time: omnipotent and yet with the limited capacity of a human being . . . [is like claiming] that a figure drawn on paper has the attributes of both a circle and square.'[27]

The notion of God and the notion of a human being are diametrically opposed, so that to say that the man Jesus is God comes very near to talking nonsense. However, mythically understood, the significance of Jesus does not lose its central place in Christianity, but can be intelligibly expressed and retained while avoiding the implications flowing from a literalist understanding.

Biblical criticism If the arguments above are accepted, they are clearly decisive, whatever the results of biblical criticism. Nevertheless, Hick finds scriptural support for his suggestions from a band of biblical exegetes in a controversial book which he edited, entitled *The Myth of God Incarnate* (1977). The thrust of Hick's argument is twofold. First, 'New Testament scholarship has shown how fragmentary and ambiguous are the data available to us', so much so that he has called Jesus 'the largely unknown man of Nazareth'.[28] Hence, there is not enough historical evidence upon which to base a claim for the divinity of Jesus and such evidence as there is shows that the historical Jesus did not make for himself the claims which the Church was later to make for him.[29] However, Hick does think that the biblical reports testify to the experience, confirmed by Christians today, that through encountering Jesus, God is also encountered – not that Jesus was God: 'That *God* has been encountered through Jesus is communicated mythologically by saying that he was God the Son incarnate.'[30] This must be seen for what it is, 'a particular redemption-myth attached to one great historical way of salvation.'[31] He argues that this understanding of Christology is becoming popular, although its implications are not always recognized.[32]

Hick maintains that if this Copernican shift and the attendant Christological suggestions are accepted, it means that the major world religions can now be seen as 'encounters from different historical and cultural standpoints with the same infinite divine reality', and thereby acknowledged as equally effective and equally valid paths to salvation.[33] Moreover, this Copernican attitude is consistent with the principle that if one's own religious experience is granted veracity, then this principle must be equally extended to the religious experience of others, be they Hindu, Buddhist or Muslim. To do otherwise would betray an unacceptable parochialism.[34]

According to Hick, this Copernican view frees the Christian for genuine dialogue and a 'mutual mission of sharing experiences and insights, mutual enrichment and . . . co-operation.'[35] The attitude of Christians to other religions need not be characterized by mistrust, desire to convert or superiority, but a will to learn and grow together towards the truth.[36]

The phenomenological arguments for Hick's Copernican revolution

Before assessing Hick's impressive theological arguments, let us look at further phenomenological considerations which he employs. In Hick's experience of people from other religions, not only did he meet saintly and holy *individuals*, but also found within the Jewish, Muslim, Hindu and Sikh *communities* meeting for worship in Birmingham, 'human beings opening their minds to a higher divine Reality, known as personal and good and as demanding righteousness and love between man and man.'[37] Hick discerned a common soteriological[38] pattern within the major religious traditions, leading adherents to 'the transformation of human existence from self-centredness to Reality-centredness.'[39]

Allied to this phenomenological observation is another simple Copernican insight about Ptolemaic theologies, be they Christian or Hindu: 'This is the fact that the particular standpoint of a Ptolemaic theology normally depends upon where the believer happens to have been born.'[40] In effect, if a person is born within a Hindu family in Madras he or she is likely to hold a Hindu Ptolemaic theology, if born to Muslim parents in Karachi, he or she is likely to hold a Muslim

Ptolemaic theology, and so on. Consequently to claim that one religion is 'partial or inferior' to another, is for Hick a form of cultural parochialism.[41]

Hick has also employed the researches of the pluralist historian, Smith. Drawing upon Smith's *The Meaning and End of Religion* (1978), to which he wrote the foreword, Hick argues that Smith's work challenges our idea of religions as mutually exclusive entities. Only in the seventeenth-century Christian West did the notion of religions as 'systems of beliefs embodied in mutually exclusive ideological communities' become accepted, replacing the prevailing assumption up to then of religion as a way of life, faith, obedience and piety.[42] Following Smith, Hick calls this personal response to the divine reality 'faith', as distinguished from the 'cumulative traditions' which are the multifarious changing historical and cultural expressions of faith.[43] This false Western conceptualization is partially responsible for our view of religions as rivals, vying with each other and making monopolistic claims to truth.[44] Hick argues that if Smith's proposed conceptual and perceptual shift is accepted, then improper questions such as 'which is the true, or truest, religion?' can be legitimately abandoned and fruitful attention paid to the diverse ways in which men and women have responded to the divine.[45]

JOHN HICK'S PLURALISM EVALUATED

What are we to make of Hick's powerful battery of theological and phenomenological arguments? However we assess them, it is clear that many of these arguments and assumptions are commonly shared, in differing degrees and various ways, by other Christian pluralists. By examining Hick in some detail, I will also deal with many of the assumptions common to the pluralist paradigm.

Theological considerations

I shall begin with the central theological tenet justifying the Copernican shift, and upon which the pluralist paradigm is based: *the universal salvific will of God*. In the following two chapters we shall see whether Hick's dismissal of the exclusivist

(Kraemer) and inclusivist (Rahner) positions is justified. I shall examine Hick's claim that they flatly contradict and implausibly explain this most important Christian axiom. However, for the moment I wish to question the sometimes misleading presentation made by Hick of an either–or, Ptolemaic–Copernican choice, whereby Ptolemaic theology is identified as one which advertently or inadvertently consigns the majority of humankind to perdition, claiming that its own 'particular faith alone has taught the truth and constituted the only effective way of salvation'.[46]

The Copernican view is presented as an alternative universalist view to this *narrow* conception of Ptolemaic theology. Faced with such a stark choice, it might well be that a Copernican revolution is required! Elsewhere, however, Hick acknowledges that inclusivist developments – a *broader* Ptolemaic view – do not confine salvation to Christians or Christianity alone.[47] The real issue here is not exclusive salvation but implausible theology. Consequently, while examining Hick's position, we should remember that the choice is not between a stark no salvation for non-Christians, as opposed to salvation for all. Until we inspect the exclusivist and inclusivist positions, let us accept Hick's suggestion (rather than requirement) for a Copernican shift and assess the coherency of this paradigm.

A major objection to this shift away from ecclesiocentricism and Christocentricism concerns the 'God' at the centre of the universe of faiths. There are two fundamental questions that arise. The first concerns the *basis* and *grounding* for the belief in the universal salvific will of the God at the centre of the universe of faiths. The second concerns this *normative theocentric* centre: surely the notion of an all-loving God accommodates only some forms of theistic religion? What of certain strands of Hinduism or Buddhism (Advaita or Theravada) where belief in a personal God is absent or denied?[48]

To begin with the first point: if the Copernican revolution requires an all-loving God as its fundamental axiom, as Hick contends, then such a claim needs grounding. I submit that it is difficult to see how Hick can avoid becoming Ptolemaic, in the broader sense, in carrying out this task. In effect, I shall argue that Hick's Christian theocentricism cannot be severed from Christology.

How does Hick ground his theocentric claim? Throughout his

career Hick has consistently argued that we cannot know God through philosophical reasoning or inference, but primarily by religious experience.[49] This emphasis on experience follows a line through to Troeltsch (a fellow pluralist), back to Schleiermacher (another pluralist) and Kant (father of the Copernican revolution in philosophy).[50] When Hick is pressed about the religious experience in which such a God is encountered, he is unequivocal that as a Christian, the assertion of an all-loving God who desires the salvation of all is grounded in the specific fact that the Christian experiences his or her own life 'in greater or lesser degree, as being lived in the presence of God, *as made known to us by Jesus*' – and in this sense Jesus is 'decisive' or 'normative' for Hick.[51]

In an earlier work Hick makes this same point more forcefully:

> It was the experience of the disciples that *God's fatherly love* was revealed in the life of Christ. Jesus told men that God loves and cares for each of them with an infinitely gracious, tender, and wise love; and the assertion was credible on his lips because this supernatural agape was apparent in his own dealings with them . . .[52]

A little later he adds, 'the event from which the Christian conception of providence is derived, is the death of Jesus Christ'.[53] Admittedly, these latter two quotes come from Hick's pre-Copernican days, but they highlight the question as to whether the attempt to sever Christology from the Christian view of God is viable or coherent. If it is not, then it would appear that Hick is himself a covert Ptolemaic theologian. If it is coherent, then Hick's Copernican revolution will both be legitimate and attractive. (A covert Ptolemaic theologian, in this instance, would be one who in trying to escape a normative Christocentricism, replaced it with a normative theocentricism, when in fact that very theocentricism relied implicitly on a form of normative Christocentricism.)

How does Hick's mythological Christology effect this question? In employing his distinction between mythical and literal incarnation, Hick is clearly trying to avoid an understanding of the incarnation as the *absolutely unique* and *only disclosure of God* to human beings, thereby demanding adherence to this single disclosure for salvation. Although he does not altogether discount the possibility of a unique disclosure, he suggests that there are 'many positive reasons . . . for thinking that this is not true'.[54] We have already seen many of his reasons, primarily the universal salvific will of God. Although Hick is trying to sever an exclusive ontological linking of Jesus and God, I would submit that his mythological understanding still maintains (implicitly, if not explicitly) a *normative* ontological linking of Jesus and God, which is in fact necessary to support his central axiom of a God of universal love. Without this premise, the Copernican enterprise will collapse. With this premise, and its inevitable *Christological* implications, the Copernican revolution looks rather like yet another ingenious Ptolemaic epicycle! I will examine Hick's arguments for a mythological understanding of the incarnation to develop this criticism further.

Other religions   Hick noted a cross-cultural natural religious tendency to exalt a human founder to an elevated divine status, thereby transposing psychological absolutes into ontological (and often exclusive) absolutes. Although, importantly, the notion of 'divinity' in the examples cited by Hick differ considerably,[55] it is necessary to guard against a particular danger arising from this observation. I believe that Hick would also wish to avoid this implication. He seems to recognize that there is a Feuerbachian note underpinning his argument: 'Feuerbach's account of the idea of God as a projection of human ideals has a certain application here', whereby the Christian projects his or her own 'spiritual needs' upon Jesus.[56] The danger is that this argument, taken to its conclusion, implies that religious language may be reduced to a subjectivist expressionism without any real reference – the emphasis being purely upon the projecting and not that upon which it is projected. Although this is not a disreputable view and is held by a number of theologians such as Don Cupitt and Richard Braithwaite, Hick has constantly rejected a non-cognitive, non-referential, non-ontological view of religious language, and has criticized both Cupitt and Braithwaite on this very point.[57]

Hick makes it clear that the believer's language concerning Jesus does express the cognitive claim that through Jesus Christians encounter the God of love: 'Of what kind is the love of

God? The Christian answer points to the love for men and women that Jesus both taught and lived out in his own life.' After all, Hick acknowledges that '"love" is a many-coloured word' and requires specification.[58] So even if the language of incarnation is mythological, it clearly has ontological import. This also has the inclusivist implication that the God of universal love requires grounding in a *normative* Christology. The God of universal love at the centre cannot be spoken of or recognized without Jesus, an implication which Hick explicitly and unjustifiably rejects when propounding his theology of religions.

Furthermore, simply because there *may* be a natural religious tendency to exalt a human founder to an exalted divine status, one cannot deny such claims *a priori* – unless Feuerbach's thesis is accepted wholeheartedly. Hence, John Rodwell is correct when he points out that 'it matters not one jot for the legitimacy of a hypothesis how it came to be formed'.[59] This surely applies to Hick's argument about a natural religious tendency invalidating the literal status of the incarnation. If Hick's argument from a general tendency in all religions to deify founders is found wanting, he still relies on other arguments. Hick has also asked that when the claim for a literal incarnation is made can its philosophical intelligibility be defended? I will now deal with this further objection.

Philosophical issues The use, meaning and status of Christological language is indeed a complex and difficult issue. Here, I only wish to pursue the criticism that Hick's myth/literal distinction does not circumvent the necessity of grounding our understanding of God in Christology – thereby undermining the Copernican premise. Let us recall Hick's example of the distinction between mythic and literal language:

> I may say of a certain happening that it is the work of the devil. If this is not literally true, the statement is mythic in character, and it is a true statement in so far as the attitude which it tends to evoke is *appropriate* to the *actual character* of the event in question.[60]

The difficulty in Hick's distinction becomes evident when we ask what constitutes an 'appropriate' response? If I were to think of such a 'happening', let us call it a motor accident, as the work of the devil in a mythical sense, in what fashion would it be appropriate to the 'actual character' of the event if it did not bear some reference to an entity or force designated 'the devil'? Or why, for instance, is it inappropriate to think of the same accident as the stupidity of a human driver or even the work of God? Does the notion of 'inappropriate' indicate the purely subjective attitude of a person to a situation without real concern for, or reference to, the 'literal' truth of the situation, its 'actual character'? If not, then mythic truth has more to do with the real character of events than simply denoting attitudes, otherwise the notion of inappropriate becomes vacuous – as does any notion of appropriate.

We approach the heart of the issue when Hick answers these questions, precisely in relation to Christology. 'If, then, the *appropriate* attitude to Jesus the Christ is the attitude of saved to saviour, how can this be justified if he is not *literally* God incarnate?' Hick answers:

> Through their responses to the person of Jesus countless people have been opened to the divine presence; changed in the direction of their lives; reconciled to themselves, to their neighbours and to God; have become conscious of the *reality* of their *loving heavenly Father* who has forgiven and accepted them ... It was not he [Jesus] but his heavenly Father who saved. But Jesus was so fully *God's agent*, so completely conscious of living in God's presence and serving God's love, that the divine reality was *mediated* through him to others.[61]

The 'appropriate' or 'practical truth' seems not to lie exclusively in the believer's subjective response, but in the 'reality' of 'God's presence ... mediated through' Jesus. Hence, an appropriate response refers to the 'real character of that which is being identified.'[62]

If Hick is saying this much, and we have already seen his disavowal of a purely subjectivist non-cognitive view of religious language, then surely he is saying too much! If Christian discourse about God takes on its coherence and appropriateness in terms of Jesus, and this discourse concerns truth, then Hick has clearly failed to sever the ontological import of Christological language. Elsewhere, he criticizes the subjectivist tones of his fellow pluralist Smith. In counter-balancing Smith's emphasis upon personal response, Hick writes:

> Just as revelation is only real when it is responded to, but on the other hand can only be responded to because it is already 'there' to be responded to, so a religion . . . can only become personalistically true in a man's life because those beliefs were already true beliefs, pointing towards and not away from the divine reality, and because those practices were already appropriate rather than inappropriate as ways in which to worship and serve the divine reality.[63]

Hick's distinction between mythic and literal runs into further difficulties when we examine his notion of literal or theoretical truth. He defines literal truth as theoretical truth and writes the following: 'A theory is true or false (or partly true and partly false); and any theory that can be of interest to human beings must be capable, in principle at least, of confirmation or disconfirmation within human experience.'[64]

Hick has consistently maintained that religious language about God can be verified, at least in principle, in the after-life. He has held this view against all forms of non-cognitive religious discourse as was earlier seen in relation to Braithwaite and Cupitt. Hence language about God has the status of theory or literal truth. But if talk of God derives from Jesus, as we have seen above, then by implication Christological language must also have some literal or theoretical truth. Hick's criticism that the incarnation is as intelligible as a square circle has been criticized for this very reason. Herbert Macabe argues that the square-circle analogy is confusing, precisely because it is not clear that God is incompatible, in his domain of activity, with man.[65] One may legitimately ask Hick to explain the meaning of his assertion that God's love is 'mediated through' Jesus in the light of his own square-circle analogy. It is this insensitivity to incarnational language which leads Nicholas Lash to notice that 'according to Hick, the fathers of Nicea unwittingly taught meaningless nonsense'.[66]

Biblical criticism   In the light of the above, I shall not pursue the biblical side of Hick's thesis as I have already shown that, on Hick's own premises, credible Christian discourse about God requires grounding in Christology. However, a number of observations may further strengthen my argument.

Norman Anderson has noted that 'Hick greatly exaggerates the paucity of positive evidence we have about the one to whom he refers as the "largely unknown man of Nazareth".'[67] Anderson goes on to show how, despite this, Hick still makes strong claims concerning Jesus' disclosure of God's presence and love which run contrary to his biblical scepticism about our knowledge of the historical Jesus. This biblical scepticism, which introduces internal strains in Hick's theology, is not shared by Knitter. After a judicious survey of New Testament Christology, Knitter comes to the conclusion that Jesus' divinity should be understood as one, and not an exclusive, occurrence of God's presence being made manifest in men and women. Unlike Hick, he recognizes that this mythological claim 'does not imply that there is no truth-content . . . no ontology at all, within early Christology'.[68]

Although clear about the ontological claims of Christology, Knitter, like Hick, fails to recognize that normative theocentricism must therefore eventually rely on normative Christocentricism.[69] Race, while disavowing Hick's biblical scepticism, embraces Troeltsch's relativism in claiming that Jesus can only be decisive for 'one cultural setting'. Knitter rightly points out that 'Race seems to end up with the "wretched historicism" and the relativism that he warns against in his analysis of Troeltsch.'[70]

The non-theistic religions and the universe of faiths   I have dwelt in some detail on Hick's Christological arguments to establish two points. First, I have maintained that Hick's pluralist axiom concerning the universal salvific will of God requires grounding in Christology.[71] Secondly, if this is true, Hick's pluralist move from Christocentricism to theocentricism is difficult to justify. If my argument is accepted, then we can also see that Hick has failed to appreciate the inclusivist and exclusivist preoccupations with the axiom which he discards: i.e. salvation is found only through the grace of God *in Christ.* In as much as Hick accepts the former part of this axiom, I have been trying to show that he must then also accept the latter part: *in Christ.* For if salvation, whether in Christianity or in other religions, comes from God, then the Christian can only assert and identify this through Christological spectacles, so to speak.

At the outset I raised two major difficulties. The first concerned the *basis* for belief in the universal salvific will of the God at the centre of the universe of faiths. Even if my reflections on this first point are rejected, there is a second major objection to Hick's Copernican revolution concerning the *normative theocentric* centre of the universe of faiths: surely the notion of an all-loving God accommodates only some forms of *theistic* religions. What then, of certain strands of non-theistic Hinduism or Buddhism? How can Hick accommodate these within his universe of faiths?[72]

Hick's response to this criticism has eventually caused him to move beyond most of his pluralist companions. At first, Hick tried to resolve this problem in a somewhat typically pluralist fashion. He rejected using mystical experience as a point of unity between the religions, as some pluralists have done, thereby denying any real differences between religions.[73] Instead, Hick adopted the approach of trying to reconcile differences in terms of a model of *complementary*, rather than *contradictory*, responses to the same divine reality.[74] He pointed out, for instance, that within the mysticism of Meister Eckhart there was 'an experience of God as other than personal within Christianity'.[75] And within non-theistic Hinduism there is also an understanding of God as personal, *Iswara*, 'who represents the Absolute as known and worshipped by finite persons'.[76]

By employing such examples, it was not altogether clear whether Hick was actually siding with the Advaitin thesis, which allowed God a provisional status, until the ultimate truth of a non-personal Absolute became apparent. Certain critics therefore accused him of being a covert Advaitin.[77]

Hick's point, although not developed in depth, was that the same infinite divine reality could be at the 'experiential roots' of the various religions, but that 'their differing experiences of that reality, inter-acting over the centuries with the different thought-forms of different cultures, have led to increasing differentiation and contrasting elaboration'.[78] Indeed, Hick argues, these very differences can be the source of further learning and renewed self-understanding in the open dialogue between religions:

Those who accept the pluralist vision are free with good
conscience to benefit from the immense spiritual values and
insights of other traditions. Thus Christians can learn to practice
the profound Hindu methods of meditation, to be fed by the
glorious faith of the Muslim Sufis and Indian *bhaktas*, and to be
illuminated by the wisdom of the Buddha . . . And corresponding
new possibilities of enrichment likewise open up for the adherents of the other great traditions.[79]

Hick, like many pluralists, is surely right in emphasizing
that there is much to be learned from other religions. A
sometimes over-anthropomorphic Christianity can admittedly
learn from the Theravadin or Advaitin denial of personal
attributes to the ultimate; similarly with matters such as
immanence and transcendence, meditation and action, silence
and praise, to name but a few polarities.[80] Incidentally, it could
be argued that many of the polarities recently located and
emphasized in inter-religious dialogue have always been
present within Christian history, in its interaction with the
various cultures of the time.[81]

However, in the words of Smith, the pluralist position
requires that 'in all ultimate matters, truth lies not in an
either–or but in a both–and'.[82] There are two difficult problems
here that must be faced. The first may be stated thus: if the
Copernican revolution requires a *God* of love at the centre for its
initial coherence, then surely, however interesting and illuminating the insights from non-theistic religions, in the final
analysis they cannot be said to be as true or as appropriate to the
divine reality. And connectedly, the second criticism may be
stated thus: the pluralist seems to view truth-claims from other
religions as *a priori partial* claims, which can then be recon-
structed within a larger pluralist complementary model. Surely
this type of dialogue can damage the integrity of the truth-
claims made by other religions in denying their status as the
ultimate claims about the way things are. The charges of
arrogance and triumphalism may curiously rebound back upon
the pluralists who direct these same charges at exclusivists.

Although truth-claims may be complementary, some may
also be contradictory.[83] For instance, given the host of im-
mensely difficult hermeneutical, linguistic, psychological and
cultural problems involved in properly understanding what a

person from another religion is saying, can we discount, *a priori* and unhistorically, genuine conflicting truth-claims? Surely it is possible that a Theravadin Buddhist, after understanding what a Christian means by 'God', may actually deny God's existence because of his or her own religious vision?[84] To discount such conflicts or castrate them by means of dissolving them within a reductive complementary system is surely a disservice to one's own religious convictions as well as that of one's partner.

It is notable that many recent pluralists are content to emphasize only the positive complementary hypothesis and not the genuine conflicting claims that can and do occur. Some have been accordingly criticized.[85]

However, let us now return to the initial objection I raised concerning this both–and model of truth, that of the theistic God at the centre of the universe of faiths.

Hick's Copernican epicycle Hick has added a number of epicycles to the Copernican revolution to meet the objection that his pluralist theology cannot accommodate non-theistic religions. In doing this, he has developed the pluralist position further than any recent exponent and has described this shift as a 'global philosophy of, or interpretation of religions'.[86] In response to the criticism that it was a Christian God at the centre of the universe of faiths, Hick introduced and developed a Kantian-type distinction between the '*noumenal* world, which exists independently, and outside man's perception of it, and the *phenomenal* world, which is that world as it appears to our human consciousness'.[87] The 'Divine Reality', 'Eternal One' or the 'Real', various terms used by Hick, occupied the centre of the universe of faiths and was analogous to the *noumenal* realm. The varying *phenomenal* responses within the different religious traditions, both theistic and non-theistic, were to be viewed as authentic but different responses to this noumenal 'Divine Reality'.

This shift, with the use of the terms 'Eternal One' and the 'Real' to designate the noumenal reality, was employed by Hick to repudiate two types of criticism. It circumvented the charge that it was the Christian God inhabiting the centre of the universe of faiths. It also allowed Hick to distinguish his position from that of the Hindu Advaita Vedanta view, which holds that God is ultimately 'non-personal . . . and that the worship of personal gods belongs to a lower and preliminary stage of the religious life which is eventually to be left behind'.[88] It also differed from the 'Visistadvaitist view that Brahman is ultimately personal'.[89] This meant that, unlike either of the Hindu views, the 'Real is *equally authentically thought* and *experienced* as personal and non-personal'.[90] Within this overall philosophical framework, Hick argues that the great world religions 'are fundamentally alike in exhibiting a soteriological structure. That is to say, they are all concerned with salvation/ liberation/enlightenment/fulfilment . . . Along each path the great transition is from the sin and error of self-enclosed existence to the liberation and bliss of Reality-centredness.'[91] In effect, this common soteriological structure can be typified as exhibiting a turning from 'self-centredness to Reality-centredness'.[92]

Hick thinks that this Copernican epicycle overcomes the criticism that a theistic God inhabits the centre of the universe of faiths, as well as allowing, understanding and explaining, genuine religious plurality. By means of this epicycle he has introduced a novel development within the pluralist paradigm, which some pluralists seem not to have recognized.[93]

Has Hick's epicycle been successful in overcoming these objections? A major difficulty arises because this epicycle, designed to overcome the charge of Christian bias, undercuts the basis for the Copernican revolution itself! We saw earlier that the foundational axiom for the Copernican revolution is the universal salvific will of God. Remove God from the centre, and substitute the 'Eternal One', and the requirements for such a Copernican shift are also removed. Why should the Christian, or anyone else, consider that all religions lead to the same divine reality? Furthermore, besides seeming to cut the ground from under his feet, there is the very real possibility that this new Copernican development in Hick's pluralist paradigm relies on agnostic presuppositions. This issue will be sharply raised when I consider Hick's contention that all the religions exhibit a common soteriological structure. I shall be asking to what these various structures point. But first it will be worth clearing the ground by dealing with less weighty phenomenological considerations put forward by Hick in support of this position.

Phenomenological considerations

If, as I have argued, Hick's theological considerations have serious internal difficulties, can he rest his case on the phenomenological considerations he has put forward?[94] The most important argument relates to the common soteriological structures that are discernible within the different religions. But first, I will briefly examine the argument that a person's place of birth determines their religion, and the argument that the distinction between faith and belief requires us to reconsider the notion that different religions make conflicting truth-claims.

Hick is surely right in pointing out that one's religion is often determined by one's birthplace. However, then to imply that because of this, all religions are equal paths to the truth tends to make truth a function of birth. This underlying assumption, which is required if the argument is to have any weight, runs into considerable difficulties. Elsewhere, Hick acknowledges this when he writes of Nazism, warlock worship and witchcraft (which could be chosen because of the family and culture into which one is born): 'To say that whatever is sincerely believed and practised is, by definition, true, would be the end of all critical discrimination, both intellectual and moral.'[95] Hick eschews this total relativization of religious truth, although admittedly some pluralists do not.[96] However, it is difficult to see how such Christian relativists would combat the claims that Nazism or witchcraft represent true responses to the divine reality.

What about Hick's adoption of Smith's distinction between 'faith' and 'cumulative traditions'? Does this distinction circumvent questions such as 'which is the true, or truest, religion?'. There is much to be said in favour of Smith's thesis: certainly the notion of competitive and rival ideological communities has led to the most barbaric persecution and hatred; and certainly within each religion there are many internal differences that sometimes render meaningless an umbrella term like Hinduism, which accommodates major theistic, non-theistic and materialist schools. Furthermore, religious life must be viewed in terms of the persons who believe and not only propositional statements of belief – which, in fact, take their meaning from the life and context of the community in which they operate. But does all this really invalidate the use of terms such as 'Christian', 'Muslim' and so on, let alone circumvent the possibility of conflicting religious truth-claims? This latter point is the real issue at stake.

I think that we can learn from Ludwig Wittgenstein's classic analysis of 'games' that we may still use a term (e.g. Christian), although the different expressions of the term have 'family resemblances' rather than a fixed and static content.[97] Allowing for exceptions, and how could exceptions or abberant types be identified otherwise, surely central paradigm cases of what it is to be a Christian involve belief in a God with reference to Jesus; for a Muslim, belief in the final authority of the Qur'an and Muhammad's words, and so on? Although we might have to say 'a Theravadin Buddhist' rather than 'a Buddhist' or an 'Advaitin' or 'Visistadvaitin' rather than a 'Hindu', the principle of a determinative paradigm with its founder, scriptures, sacred traditions, teachings and practices uniting a community of believers is surely necessary if language and religious and cultural identity are to retain any meaning at all.[98]

Given this, and Hick's support of religious language as cognitively referential, Hugo Meynell's criticism of Smith's pluralist thesis is pertinent:

> Once the chips are down, all differences in expression due to culture and intellectual development taken into account, and all ambiguities removed [at least in principle – I would add], there cannot both be and not be a God; and the Qur'an bestowed through Muhammad both be and not be the final and culminating expression by him of his nature and will to humankind . . . so long as the religious believer actually believes anything, as opposed to merely having a set of aesthetic or practical attitudes, he is inevitably *liable* to this kind of disagreement with other religious believers and unbelievers. Vague talk of a 'transcendent' to which all religious believers are committed conceals rather than disposes of this awkward fact.[99]

Although Meynell's final comment about vague talk of a 'transcendent' was aimed at Smith, might the same be said of Hick's 'Eternal One' or 'Real'? Hick's distinction between the noumenal and phenomenal reinforces this suspicion, and I now return to the objection I raised earlier concerning the possible agnostic presuppositions in Hick's Copernican epicycle.

We are finally and inevitably led to the most important of Hick's phenomenological considerations: that all religions have similar soteriological structures, facilitating a turning from 'self-centredness to Reality-centredness'. To speak of salvation as a turning from self-centredness to Reality-centredness certainly removes any Ptolemaic linguistic echoes, but it is also in danger of removing any substantial content to the notion of salvation and the different religious truth-claims, by collapsing and assimilating them together as 'Reality-centred'. David Hume's comment on mystics and their claims may be equally applied to Hick's noumenal reality: 'Is the name, without any meaning, of such mighty importance? Or how do MYSTICS, who maintain the absolute incomprehensibility of the deity, differ from sceptics or atheists . . .?'[100] A number of recent critics have pointed out that Hick's distinction between the noumenal and phenomenal, in the words of one of them, 'is very close to unbelief'.[101] Kant's noumenon encountered the same problem: how can Kant 'claim to know that there is a correspondence between phenomena and things in themselves, and that the latter act upon consciousness?'.[102]

Hick tries to steer clear of such an agnosticism or unbelief as it is his contention that the various religions are equally valid and real salvific apprehensions of the one divine noumenal reality. He further argues that the truth of the various religions can only be decided through eschatological verification. It is only in the after-life that such questions can be answered.[103] But it is precisely the introduction of this final epicyclic escape route that poses yet another objection to Hick's Copernican revolution. Philip Almond has asked whether it is 'reasonable to demand a Copernican revolution . . . while the possibility remains that, in the final eschatological analysis, it *may* turn out that a Ptolemaic Christian view of some sort or other was theologically valid?'[104] Almond does not pursue this charge, but could have if he had turned to Hick's own eschatological speculations in *Death and Eternal Life*. The charge I wish to pursue is that Hick *has* in fact carried out such an 'eschatological analysis' – and the eschaton (the final state of affairs) is quite definitely theistic, if not altogether Christian! And some such conclusion is necessary if the notion of Reality-centredness is not to remain vacuous.

In two important works published since his Copernican shift, *Death and Eternal Life* (1976) and an essay in *Encountering Evil* (1981), Hick's 'Eternal One' is seen to be, come the eschaton, a theistic God at the *end*, rather than at the *centre* of the universe of faiths in loving communion with all humankind. He describes his own position as one which 'depicts persons as still in the course of creation towards an end-state of perfected personal community in the divine kingdom. This end-state is conceived as one in which individual egoity has been transcended in communal unity before God.'[105] We should also notice his admission, in these works, that this position requires a 'conception of God as personal Lord, distinct from his creation'.[106] Furthermore, he acknowledges that this eschatological view 'implicitly rejects the *advaitist* view that atman *is* Brahman, the collective human self being ultimately identical with God'.[107]

If this is the case, then Hick seems to hold two contradictory positions. First, both theistic and non-theistic religions are equally salvific in value and the 'Real is *equally authentically thought and experienced* as personal and non-personal' [my italics]. Secondly, and to my mind incompatibly, he holds that our final (and therefore presumably true) relation to the 'Real' is one of eternal loving communion with a personalist, all-loving God. If this is so, on what grounds can it be asserted that the non-personalist, non-theistic religions are as equally authentic and true as the personalist, theistic ones? Will not the Advaitin, Theravadin Buddhist and adherent to Samkhya Yoga all find that their *thought* and *experience* of 'the Real' was not equally as authentic or appropriate as that found within the personalist religions?

At this point Hick may reply that in the eschatological process he has allowed for the possibility of the correction, enlargement or transformation of different religious dogmas.[108] The Advaitin, for example, would only gradually come to recognize the way 'things are' in the course of many after-lives. However, if Hick were to pursue this path, we would then have to ask how he can claim that these non-theistic religions, as they *now* exist, are equally salvific and equally true in their beliefs and experience? Are they salvific despite their beliefs and experience? And if their beliefs and experience are not appropriate to the 'Eternal One', as revealed in the eschaton, what is to be made of the notion that all religions exhibit a common soteriological structure?

My contention has been that if Hick's theistic God is removed from the *centre* of the universe of faiths through the epicycle just considered, we find that in the final 'eschatological analysis' a theistic God reappears at the *end* of the universe of faiths, once more pushing Hick back into the Ptolemaic camp from which he is trying to escape. I have tried to show how both his theological and phenomenological considerations are open to grave objections, often betraying an underlying form of inclusivism or alternatively giving way to a confusing and reductive agnosticism.

CONCLUSION

In this detailed examination of a major pluralist advocate I have tried to isolate and examine certain theological and phenomenological assumptions, often common to other pluralists. By pointing out some serious difficulties within the pluralist paradigm, I have sometimes neglected many of the positive and valuable contributions made by pluralists. They rightly stress the axiom of the universal salvific will of God, while sometimes rejecting the basis for this axiom: that God's universal salvific will is made known in and through Christ. Furthermore, they raise serious questions, as yet unresolved, about the exclusivist and inclusivist paradigms. They also rightly stress that dialogue needs to be free of superiority or chauvinism and characterized by mutual enrichment, sharing and cooperation. However, they often neglect the confessional and proclamatory elements of dialogue. Indeed, they raise questions as to whether these two sides of dialogue are in fact compatible. They also offer a theological framework for a positive appraisal of non-Christian communities and their scriptures, practices and beliefs. Unfortunately, this framework raises major problems. Do the exclusivist and inclusivist views necessarily lead to the denigration of the non-Christian scriptures, beliefs and practices? Pluralists further alert us to the complicated difficulties in assessing and determining questions of religious truth. At the same time they sometimes neglect the implications of their own proposals, or too excessively stress a complementary model of truth-claims as against the possibility of genuinely conflicting and differing truth-claims.

If we have good reasons to be dissatisfied with the pluralist approach, do the exclusivist or inclusivist paradigms more satisfactorily attend to the deficiencies within the pluralist position? And if they do, can they include many of the positive insights and contributions put forward by pluralists? I shall further pursue these questions in the next chapter by examining the thought of the exclusivist theologian Hendrik Kraemer.

NOTES

1. For surveys see P. Knitter, *No Other Name? A Critical Survey of Christian Attitudes Towards the World Religions* (1985), ch. 8; A. Race, *Christians and Religious Pluralism* (1983), ch. 4. Against Knitter, I would not consider Panikkar and Samartha pluralists, and here Race is in agreement (*Pluralism* pp. 47, 59). Against Race, I would not consider Tillich a pluralist, and here Knitter is in agreement (*No Other Name?*, p. xiii).
2. Knitter, *No Other Name?*, p. 147. On p. 246 Knitter equates theocentricism with pluralism.
3. Within Judaism see D. Cohn-Sherbok, 'Judaism and the Universe of Faiths', *New Blackfriars*, 65 (1984), pp. 28–35; within Islam see H. Askari and J. Hick (eds), *The Experience of Religious Diversity* (1985).
4. I shall consider the theologies of Race, Knitter and Smith. See my paper 'An examination of the pluralist paradigm in the Christian theology of religion', *Scottish Journal of Theology*, 39 (1986) for a more detailed analysis of these three theologians.
5. J. Hick, *God has Many Names* (1980), pp. 2–3.
6. Ibid., p. 5.
7. Hick, *Universe of Faiths*, p. 131.
8. Ibid., p. 121.
9. Hick, 'Religious pluralism' in F. Whaling (ed.), *The World's Religious Traditions: Current Perspectives in Religious Studies* (1984), p. 153.
10. Hick, *God has Many Names* (US edn; 1982), p. 27.
11. Hick, *Universe of Faiths*, p. 126.
12. Hick, *World's Religious Traditions*, p. 153.
13. Hick, *Universe of Faiths*, p. 131.
14. Hick, *World's Religious Traditions*, p. 153.
15. Hick, *Universe of Faiths*, p. 131.

16. Ibid., p. 122.
17. See also Knitter, *No Other Name?*, p. 140 and ch. 8; Race, *Pluralism*, ch. 4; A. Toynbee, *Christianity Among the Religions of the World* (1957), p. 111; W. C. Smith, *Towards a World Theology* (1980), p. 171, *The Faith of Other Men* (1972), p. 138.
18. See, for example, M. Green (ed.), *The Truth of God Incarnate* (1977), ch. 1, 2, 4, 5; J. N. Anderson, *The Mystery of the Incarnation* (1978), ch. 3; J. Lipner, 'Christians and the uniqueness of Christ', *Scottish Journal of Theology*, 28 (1976), pp. 359–68. Knitter, *No Other Name?*, p. 167, and Race, *Pluralism*, p. 106, acknowledge Christology to be the main problem facing the pluralist position.
19. Hick, *God has Many Names* (US), p. 58.
20. Ibid.
21. Hick (ed.), *The Myth of God Incarnate* (1977), pp. 168–70; and the same can be said of Mithras, Rama, Krishna, Durga, Kali – Hick, *Universe of Faiths*, pp. 172, 178. Knitter offers a similar argument based on the historical–cultural context of the New Testament – *No Other Name?*, pp. 182ff.
22. Hick, *God has Many Names* (US), p. 57; *The Second Christianity* (1983), p. 32; and Knitter, *No Other Name?*, p. 185.
23. Hick, *Universe of Faiths*, pp. 166ff; *God has Many Names*, pp. 70ff.
24. Hick, *Universe of Faiths*, p. 167.
25. Ibid.
26. Ibid., p. 172.
27. Hick, *Second Christianity*, p. 31.
28. Hick, *Myth*, pp. 116–17.
29. Knitter disagrees with Hick's historical–biblical scepticism (*No Other Name?*, pp. 174ff), as does Race (*Pluralism*, pp. 123ff).
30. Hick, *Universe of Faiths*, p. 172.
31. Ibid., p. 177.
32. Hick cites the Christologies of D. and J. Baillie, G. Lampe, N. Pittenger, J. Knox (*World's Religious Traditions*, pp. 154–5), and, of course, the contributors to *Myth*. Knitter adds to this list Rahner and Process Christologies in *No Other Name?*, pp. 186ff.
33. Hick, *Universe of Faiths*, p. 141.
34. Hick, *World's Religious Traditions*, p. 157; Hick, *Why Believe in God?* (with M. Goulder, 1983) ch. 2, 6; for this same argument see Knitter, *No Other Name?*, p. 228; Smith, *World Theology*, p. 101; Race, *Pluralism*, pp. 5–6.
35. Hick, *World's Religious Traditions*, p. 164.
36. Hick, *God has Many Names* (US), ch. 7; for similar criticisms of dialogue see Knitter, *No Other Name?*, p. 134; Race, *Pluralism*, pp. 145ff; Smith, *World Theology*, p. 96.
37. Hick, *God has Many Names*, p. 5.

38. The word 'soteriology' is derived from the Greek *Soteria*, salvation. Hick is thereby indicating a common salvific pattern.
39. Hick, 'On grading religions', *Religious Studies*, 17 (1981), p. 452.
40. Hick, *Universe of Faiths*, p. 132.
41. Ibid.
42. Smith argues this is true of all religions except Islam.
43. Hick, *World's Religious Traditions*, p. 148. In this same essay Hick points out that he is not totally satisfied with Smith's proposals.
44. Hick, *Universe of Faiths*, p. 101; *World's Religious Traditions*, pp. 147ff.
45. In W. C. Smith, *The Meaning and End of Religion: A New Approach to the Religious Traditions of Mankind* (1978).
46. Hick, 'The theology of religious pluralism', *Theology*, 86 (1983), pp. 335–40.
47. Hick, *God has Many Names*, pp. 49ff.
48. These two objections equally apply to Knitter's approval of an 'evolution from ecclesiocentricism to a christocentricism to theocentricism' (*No Other Name?*, p. 166), in the work of pluralists such as himself and those mentioned in ch. 8 of his book. See also Race, *Pluralism*, ch. 5; Smith, *World Theology*, p. 171.
49. Hick, *World's Religious Traditions*, p. 157; *Universe of Faiths*, ch. 3, 6; *The Philosophy of Religion* (1st edn, 1964), p. 30, (2nd edn 1973), p. 30.
50. Many of Hick's fellow pluralists also place much emphasis on religious experience: Troeltsch, Hocking, Smith and Race.
51. Hick, 'Pluralism and the reality of the transcendent', *Christian Century*, 98 (1981), pp. 46–7 (my italics).
52. Hick, *Faith and Knowledge* (1978), p. 225.
53. Ibid., p. 233.
54. Hick, 'The theology', p. 338.
55. See Anderson, *Mystery of the Incarnation*, ch. 3; L. Newbigin, *The Finality of Christ* (1969), pp. 50ff. For two especially good studies distinguishing the differences between *avatar* and incarnation, see G. Parrinder, *Avatar and Incarnation* (1970); Robinson, *Truth is Two-Eyed*, ch. 3.
56. Hick, *Myth*, p. 168.
57. D. Cupitt, *Taking Leave of God* (1980), *The World to Come* (1982); R. Braithwaite, *An Empiricist's View of the Nature of Religious Belief* (1955). For Hick's criticism of Braithwaite, see *The Philosophy* (1st edn), pp. 90–3; on Cupitt, *Why Believe?*, pp. 102–11. At this point Hick and Knitter part company with Race, who seems to adopt a non-cognitive view of language

(*Pluralism*, p. 127), and possibly Smith (Hick (ed.), *Truth and Dialogue* (1974), pp. 145–8).

58. Hick, *Second Christianity*, p. 39.
59. Hick, in M. Goulder (ed.), *Incarnation and Myth: The Debate Continued* (1979), p. 68.
60. Hick, *Universe of Faiths*, p. 167 (my italics).
61. Ibid., pp. 176–7 (my italics).
62. Ibid., p. 176. Consequently, N. Lash's charge against Hick's 'subjectivism' is incorrect, *Incarnation and Myth*, p. 21, but could be applied to Race's and Troeltsch's positions.
63. Hick, *Truth and Dialogue*, p. 146.
64. Hick, *Universe of Faiths*, p. 166.
65. H. Macabe, 'Review of *The Myth of God Incarnate*', *New Blackfriars* 58 (1977), p. 353. See also Hick, *Incarnation and Myth*, 2B, 3B.iv.
66. Hick, *Incarnation and Myth*, p. 22.
67. Anderson, *Mystery of the Incarnation*, p. 64.
68. Knitter, *No Other Name?*, p. 184.
69. See my 'Review of *No Other Name?*', *Modern Theology*, 2, 1 (1985), pp. 83–6.
70. Knitter, *No Other Name?*, pp. 81–2.
71. H. Willmer makes this point succinctly in C. Moule, *The Origins of Christology* (1977), p. 166.
72. See, for instance, J. Lipner, 'Does Copernicus help?', *Religious Studies*, 13 (1977), pp. 243–58; D. Forrester, 'Professor Hick and the universe of faiths', *Scottish Journal of Theology*, 29 (1976), pp. 65–72.
73. See W. James, *The Varieties of Religious Experience* (1977), s.16, 17; and S. Radhakrishnan, *A Hindu View of Life* (1927), ch. 2; and possibly even Smith, as Knitter has noted in *No Other Name?*, pp. 44–7.
74. See also Knitter, who says 'The world religions, in all their amazing differences, are more complementary than contradictory', *No Other Name?*, p. 220; Race, *Pluralism*, p. 148; Smith, *Faith of Other Men*, p. 17. N. Smart, *Beyond Ideology* (1981), p. 14, ch. 2, pp. 309ff, also seems to adopt this view of the relation between religions.
75. Hick, *Universe of Faiths*, p. 144.
76. Ibid.
77. For instance, see Forrester, 'Professor Hick and the universe of faiths', p. 69; P. Byrne, 'John Hick's philosophy of religion', *Scottish Journal of Theology*, 35 (1982), pp. 289–301.
78. Hick, *Universe of Faiths*, p. 146.
79. Hick, *Second Christianity*, p. 90.
80. See N. Smart, *The Yogi and the Devotee: The Interplay between*

the Upanishads and Catholic Theology (1968), ch. 5, and *Beyond Ideology*, ch. 6, for a fruitful discussion of these polarities.

81. See J. Newman's masterly account in *An Essay on the Development of Christian Doctrine* (1906), which stresses how Church practice, liturgy and discipline (and not only beliefs) were affected. Or again, see Aquinas's doctrine of analogy to safeguard against anthropocentricism – E. Mascall, *Existence and Analogy* (1949).

82. Smith, *Faith of Other Men*, p. 17; and Hick, *Second Christianity*, pp. 85ff.

83. See W. Christian, *Oppositions of Religious Doctrines* (1972), where he develops this point with useful examples and philosophical lucidity.

84. See, for example, G. Dharmasiri, *A Buddhist Critique of the Christian Concept of God* (1974).

85. On Smith, but relevant to other pluralists, see H. Meynell, 'The idea of a world theology', *Modern Theology*, 1 (1985), pp. 149–63; W. Wainwright, 'Wilfred Cantwell Smith on faith and belief', *Religious Studies*, 20 (1984), pp. 353–67.

86. Personal letter to the author, 2 May 1985. Significantly, ch. 6 of Hick, *God has Many Names* (US) is entitled 'Towards a philosophy of religious pluralism'. *Theology* is not perhaps so appropriate a term for Hick's epicycle, see below.

87. Hick, *God has Many Names* (US), p. 105 (my italics).

88. Ibid. p. 110.

89. Hick, 'The theology', p. 337.

90. Ibid. (my italics).

91. Hick, *Second Christianity*, pp. 86–7.

92. Hick, 'On grading', p. 467.

93. Thus, Knitter's confusing classification of Hick as 'theocentric', see *No Other Name?*, p. 147.

94. Gerard Loughlin has argued that Hick's case rests on phenomenological considerations and not theological arguments: 'Paradigms and paradox: Defending the case for a revolution in the theology of religions', *New Blackfriars*, 66 (1985), pp. 127–34.

95. Hick, *Truth and Dialogue*, p. 148. Interestingly, this criticism is aimed at Smith.

96. Smith, Race and Troeltsch.

97. See L. Wittgenstein, *Philosophical Investigations* (1958), I para. 66, and G. D'Costa, 'Elephants, ropes and a theology of religions', *Theology*, 68 (1985), pp. 259–68, where I develop this point further.

98. Hick seems to accept this, both in his use of language and in an essay in *Universe of Faiths*, ch. 8.

99. Meynell, 'Idea of World Theology', p. 154 (my comment in brackets and my italics).
100. D. Hume, *Dialogues Concerning Natural Religion* (1970), para. 1, part 4.
101. Byrne, 'Hick's philosophy of religion', p. 301; and D. Cupitt, review of Hick, *God has Many Names*, *Times Literary Supplement*, 8 August 1980, p. 902; R. Trigg, 'Religion and the threat of relativism', *Religious Studies*, 19 (1983), p. 303.
102. A. Wedberg, *A History of Philosophy*, vol. 2 (1982), p. 174.
103. Hick, 'The Theology', p. 338; *Universe of Faiths*, pp. 35–6, ch. 13. Race also adopts this eschatological manoeuvre to justify his pluralist stance; see *Pluralism*, p. 146. Knitter disavows an eschatological test but replaces it with an equally problematic Jungian criterion – see below, pp. 70–1, 134.
104. P. Almond, 'John Hick's Copernican theology', *Theology*, 66 (1983), pp. 39–40 (my italics).
105. Hick, 'An Irenaean Theodicy', in S. Davis (ed.), *Encountering Evil* (1981), p. 51.
106. Hick, *Death and Eternal Life* (1976), p. 464.
107. Ibid.
108. Hick, 'The theology', p. 338.

CHAPTER 3

The Exclusivist Paradigm

The exclusivist paradigm has been characterized as maintaining that other religions are marked by humankind's fundamental sinfulness and are therefore erroneous, and that Christ (or Christianity) offers the only valid path to salvation. This view is maintained against pluralist and inclusivist positions.

In chapter 1 we saw how the imposing theology of Hendrik Kraemer formulated and firmly established this approach. It has been written, not without exaggeration, 'that no attempt to estimate the direction of present day thought can be made without a special consideration of Kraemer's position'.[1] Even in his own time, Kraemer's importance was prophetically recognized when William Temple wrote of Kraemer's major work, *The Christian Message in a Non-Christian World* (1938): 'It is likely to remain for many years to come the classical treatment of its theme.'[2]

This exclusivist stance is adopted by many today, often within the evangelical tradition, although there is considerable diversity and debate between exponents sharing this paradigm.[3]

As in the previous chapter, I shall examine in some detail the position of my representative exclusivist theologian, Hendrik Kraemer, while also indicating similarities and differences between Kraemer and other exclusivists. This approach should facilitate a more penetrating study than would a systematic survey of the different forms of exclusivism. It is also my intention to develop a dialogue between the pluralist and exclusivist positions, highlighting and teasing out the issues relevant to formulating a Christian theology of religions.

HENDRIK KRAEMER'S EXCLUSIVISM

Hendrik Kraemer was born in Amsterdam, Holland, on 17 May 1888. His life was punctuated by much suffering and hardship: the death of his father and mother before he was thirteen; life in a strict Protestant orphanage, where he was introduced to Christianity and the Bible; and a number of nervous breakdowns in later life, the most severe in 1932. His academic career began in Leiden, where he trained as an orientalist and missionary for the Dutch Bible Society. He then went to Java to assist in the Indonesian mission fields (1922–8, 1930–6), and became well acquainted with many leading ecumenical figures. It was through these contacts that Kraemer became involved in the International Missionary Council Conferences in Jerusalem (1928) and, more significantly, in Tambaram (1938). For this latter Council he was asked to prepare a study document stating 'the fundamental position of the Christian Church as a witness-bearing body in the modern world . . . dealing in detail with the evangelistic approach to the great non-Christian faiths.'[4] He produced *The Christian Message in a Non-Christian World*, which 'caused more profound thinking on the very basis of the missionary enterprise than any book written for many years'.[5]

In the continental tradition of Barth's dialectical theology, and in sharp reaction to liberal theological trends, especially from America, Kraemer powerfully stated his position in the light of one fundamental tenet that determined his whole approach: 'God has revealed *the* Way and *the* Life and *the* Truth in Jesus Christ and wills this to be known through all the world.'[6]

After many years of missionary experience, Kraemer returned to Leiden as Professor of the History and Phenomenology of Religions (1937–48). He was imprisoned during the Second World War for his part in the resistance movement, and in 1948, at the close of the war, he became Director of the Ecumenical Institute of the World Council of Churches (1948–55). Kraemer then wrote another huge, more nuanced statement of his earlier position in *Religion and the Christian Faith* (1956). He felt this book was a clarification and re-statement, rather than a change of his basic position first expressed in *The Christian Message in a Non-Christian World*.[7] Kraemer also lectured in the United States and as a result published *The Communication of the Christian Faith* (1957) and *World Cultures and World Religions* (1960). Until his death in 1965 he lived in Drieberg, Holland.[8] It was during this period in Drieberg that he wrote *Why Christianity of All Religions?* (1959).

To understand Kraemer's theology, the following factors should be kept in mind: his practical, scholarly and experiential contact with the major world religions; his training as a historian of religions and phenomenologist, linguist and theologian; his constant fear of the relativizing influences of liberal theology; and his pastoral and evangelistic commitment to the ecumenical movement.

Phenomenological considerations

As an evangelical Christian and professionally trained phenomenologist, Kraemer perceived a number of advantages and disadvantages in the growing attention to historical and philosophical studies of the major world religions. He welcomed this expansion of knowledge and was wary of uninformed condemnation or praise of non-Christian religions. He also firmly opposed any cultural or imperialistic feelings of superiority when evaluating non-Christian religions. Unlike Barth, Kraemer thought that knowledge and experience of other religions were essential for evangelization and dialogue. Barth's famous reply typifies his stance. When asked how he knew that Hinduism was unbelief when he had never met a Hindu, his immediate reply was '*a priori*'![9]

If, as we have seen, the charge of superiority has been aimed at exclusivists by pluralists, Kraemer turns the charge on its head by directing this same criticism at Troeltsch. When Troeltsch maintained the relative absoluteness of Christianity, Kraemer argued that he was 'giving expression to his innate feeling of western cultural achievement',[10] because he turned his 'predilection for *personalism* into the criterion for all religions', relegating impersonal religions to a secondary place and implicitly 'assuming the superiority of Christianity as self-evident, pretending, however, to prove it'.[11] Kraemer's contention, which may at first shock liberal ears, is that Christianity, like the non-Christian religions, is a 'combination of sublime and abject elements', and a Christian phenomenologist 'will feel deeply that to speak glibly of the superiority of Christianity is offensive'.[12]

Kraemer also welcomed the recognition among some phenomenologists of what he called the *totalitarian* character of religion – that is, each religion must be analysed and understood in terms of its particular apprehension of the totality of existence.[13] Because of the totalitarian character of all religions, Kraemer objected to the isolation of surface similarities between religions, so often used by pluralists to demonstrate points of contact, similarity and continuities among the different religions. Take, for instance, Hick and Knitter's assertion that there is a common reality behind the terms *dukkha* and sin.[14] Kraemer objects to these abstract comparisons because

> Every religion is a living, indivisible unity. Every part of it – a dogma, a rite, a myth, an institution, a cult – is so vitally related to the whole that it can never be understood in its real function, significance and tendency, as these occur in the reality of life, without keeping constantly in mind the vast and living unity of existential apprehension in which this part moves and has its being.[15]

Hence, even the Buddhist and Christian notion of 'transience' cannot be easily assimilated because 'Buddhist transiency has meaning only on the background of a void, God-less universe', whereas in Christianity 'the transience of men [is understood] on the background of a real world', created and sustained by God.[16] Kraemer offers many penetrating criticisms of often-used similarities. If doctrines and ideas are interpreted out of their totalitarian context, without due regard to the complex web of beliefs and practices, they are liable to distortion. Furthermore, he insists that this kind of hermeneutical sensitivity is necessary, for interpretation is not a purely intellectual exercise. Because of the existential nature of religion, a fair amount of 'imaginative activity' is required as well as the necessary intellectual skills.[17]

The phenomenological point that Kraemer is making is not a complete denial of any similarities and points of contact, but the need for extreme caution and care – often lacking in pluralist analysis. However, as we shall see shortly, Kraemer does have theological reasons for denying such points of contact.

Kraemer's other major contention concerning phenomenological study is that it cannot provide criteria for evaluating
truth, but can only facilitate the dispassionate assembling of
data – linguistic, anthropological, historical and so on, which is
to be welcomed. Some scholars then introduce evaluative
criteria, such as a particular type of mystical experience
(Radhakrishnan), personalism (Troeltsch), pragmatism
(James), the philosophical concept of the essence of religion
(Harnack) – and we may add a Jungian psychological whole-
ness (Knitter), and a turning from self-centredness to Reality-
centredness (Hick). Kraemer does not as such object to the
introduction of such criteria, but to the view that these criteria
are either neutral or universally acceptable. As a Christian, he
argues that his own starting point, or truth criterion, is, and can
only be, the revelation and self-disclosure of God in Jesus
Christ. His contention is that this starting point for evaluation
is, in principle, as legitimate as any other.

We may now appropriately turn to Kraemer's theological
consideration of the Christian attitude to non-Christian
religions.

Theological considerations

Kraemer's attitude to the non-Christian religions is determined
by his emphasis on the axiom often minimized or neglected by
pluralists: that salvation is found only through the grace of God
revealed in Christ. This revelation is also the only possible truth
criterion for Kraemer and other exclusivists, because here alone
God has revealed himself, and only God and not human-made
norms, can judge:

> I propose to set the religions, including Christianity, in the light
> of the Person of Jesus Christ, who is the Revelation of God and
> alone has the authority to criticize – I mean, to judge discrimi-
> nately and with complete understanding – every religion and
> everything that is in man or proceeds from him.[18]

To accept the authority of this revelation, to accept what
Kraemer calls biblical realism, involves a number of implic-
ations which cannot be avoided and which determine a
Christian's attitude to the non-Christian religions.

The missionary imperative The first and foremost implication flowing from Kraemer's notion of biblical realism is the serious acceptance of the biblical witness. This means that the most essential questions about humankind and God are only answerable 'in the light of the revelation in Christ'.[19] Consequently, passages such as John 14:6 and Acts 4:12 must be taken absolutely seriously: 'I am the way, the truth and the life, no one comes to the Father but by me'; 'And there is salvation in no one else, for there is no other name under heaven given among men by which we must be saved'. Because the truth about God and humankind is revealed only in Christ, the Christian is obliged to proclaim this message to all people: 'God has revealed *the* Way and *the* Life and *the* Truth in Jesus Christ and wills this to be known throughout the world.'[20]

Kraemer criticizes those pluralists who replace this primary obligation to truth in their interpretation of mission exclusively in terms of social service or mutual enrichment. He recognizes that these latter emphases are sometimes an understandable reaction against imperialistic, 'rabid and narrow-minded proselytism'.[21] In fact, Kraemer, unlike some exclusivists, fully supports the necessity of *indigenization*: 'There is an obligation to strive for the presentation of the Christian truth in terms and modes of expression that make its challenge intelligible and related to the peculiar quality of reality in which they [non-Christians] live.'[22]

To reduce mission to service and sharing, however, obscures the demand of the Gospel that Christ be preached and accepted by all nations. Kraemer makes it clear that service and sharing are not accessories or unimportant, but directly flow from the demands of the Gospel — 'the spontaneous and indispensable *expressions* of the new mind in Christ'.[23] The 'new mind in Christ' must be the main aim of mission, otherwise Christians unconsciously adopt relativist, pragmatist or humanist conceptions of truth with painful infidelity to Christ's revelation.[24]

Against some often misdirected charges levelled by pluralists against Kraemer, it must be emphatically stated that Kraemer constantly and consistently accepts the following as concomitant with the exclusivist position: practical cooperation — medical, educational and social service; religious tolerance when it means 'that everybody should have a fair chance to present his case, but not that nobody should ardently believe in his case';[25]

an openness and willingness to learn from non-Christian religions which 'contain a great deal which really does have something to say to us and give to us'.[26]

Admittedly Kraemer is more broadminded than some exclusivists.[27] It is important to realize, however, that an attitude of superiority and non-cooperation is not concomitant with exclusivism, as some pluralists contend.

Dialectical evaluation of religions   According to Kraemer, it is necessary to understand the revelation of God's will and humankind's nature through Jesus Christ, if we are to appreciate his evaluation of all religions, Christianity included. This revelation gives access to two irreducible insights. The first is the fallenness of men and women: 'The Bible describes this inexplicable but patent fact with the words that man wanted to be "like God". Man, whose natural relation to God, His Lord and Maker, is obedience and love, has become a rebel.'[28]

This means that all people constantly try to justify themselves by means of false absolutes and human-made systems; in effect, by idolatry.[29] In Christianity this type of idolatry, according to Kraemer, is apparent in the supposed 'inerrant doctrinal authority of the Church and the infallibility of the Bible';[30] or when it is taught that salvation comes through works and not by faith alone.[31] In the non-Christian religions even the 'highest flights, the sincerest contrition, remain in the sphere of a lofty moralism or spirituality. Nowhere do we find a radical repudiation of every possible *man-made* spiritual world, which is the uncanny power of the gospel.'[32]

Although Kraemer's assessment of religion is solely the result of his theological reflections, he substantiates this contention by analysing the major non-Christian religions. He concludes by arguing that ultimately they are all human constructions of self-justification.[33] According to Kraemer, this is why the Bible says that men and women wanted to be 'like God'. Whenever a person does not submit to Christ and totally surrender to the mercy of God, revealed in Christ, however lofty and sincere his or her religion, the fundamental disobedience of humankind is reasserted.

This theological starting point is also the reason why Kraemer rejects the notion of points of contact, continuity or natural theology. Natural theology, as used here, denotes the process whereby persons can, by their own natural rational powers, arrive at a belief in God. According to Kraemer, the notion of natural theology is a rationalist divinization of reason. Furthermore, the points of contact and continuity are all irrelevant in the light of Christ's judgement upon all religions. He also argues that any notion of general revelation renders unnecessary the event of the incarnation.[34] Under the searchlight of Christ, 'all religious life, the lofty and degraded, appear to lie under the divine judgement, because it is *misdirected*'.[35] Kraemer also argues that this condemnation and questioning of the religious life of humankind in the light of the revelation of Christ 'is an indirect indication of its special and *sui generis* quality and significance'.[36]

Some exclusivists remain content with this entirely negative assessment of the non-Christian religions, and certainly Kraemer thought that Barth stopped here – undialectically.[37] However, Kraemer contends that if Christ brings judgement upon a fallen humankind, he also brings mercy and forgiveness to a humanity seeking for God. Kraemer contends that if these poles are not kept together, we get, on the one hand, a harsh and undialectical exclusivism like that of the early Barth, and on the other, an indiscriminate pluralism which compromises the question of truth. We have seen in chapter 2 that Kraemer's suspicions are not groundless.

Complementing the 'No' of judgement against all religion as forms of self-justification, is a 'Yes', because of God's faithfulness and humankind's constant, although misdirected, search. Kraemer succinctly characterizes this dialectical evaluation when he writes: 'By "dialectical" is meant this condition, inherent in man, of saying at the same time yes and no to his true destiny and his relatedness to the eternal.'[38]

Kraemer acknowledged, although not as emphatically as in his earlier books, that 'undeniably God works and has worked in man outside the sphere of biblical revelation'.[39] 'Even in this fallen world', he writes, 'God shines through in a broken, troubled way: in reason, in nature and in history.'[40] For lack of a better term, Kraemer is willing to call these happenings general revelation, with the proviso that such revelation can only be effectively discerned in the light of the 'special revelation' of Jesus Christ.[41] Furthermore, the term 'revelation' for these events should not suggest an equal or comparative status to the *sui generis* character of Christ's revelation.

In chapter 2 it was noted how criteria for discerning the action of God were necessary. Here we see how Kraemer, in company with the majority of exclusivists, refuses to move away from the incarnation as the only valid criterion for discerning the activity of God in history and upon which to base talk of God's presence in other religions. I have already noted the consequences of the pluralist strategies to abandon or relativize this normative criterion.

The other positive aspect of this dialectical evaluation lies in what Kraemer calls 'religious consciousness' (and what Calvin calls '*sensus divinitatis*').[42] Kraemer's contention, supported by phenomenological analysis is that the only common denominator behind the bewildering plurality of religions is the 'universal religious consciousness in man'.[43] This (misguided) striving after the Absolute is nevertheless a result of a genuine searching, prompted by God's creation of men and women in his own image.

As a result of this dialectical evaluation, Kraemer's answer to the question of the Christian attitude to non-Christian religions is a mixture of both 'No' and 'Yes':

> The religious and moral life of man is man's achievement, but also God's wrestling with him; it manifests a receptivity to God, but at the same time an inexcusable disobedience and blindness to God ... Man seeks God and at the same time flees from Him in his seeking, because his self-assertive self-centredness of will, his root-sin, always breaks through.[44]

HENDRIK KRAEMER'S EXCLUSIVISM EVALUATED

Kraemer's theology of religions is clearly opposed to the pluralist theologies we have already examined. Some of what Kraemer says is echoed in my criticisms of John Hick and other pluralist theologians. I shall now turn to an evaluation of Kraemer's powerful exclusivist contribution in order to maintain a dialogue with the issues raised by the pluralists.

Phenomenological considerations

One of Kraemer's most important contributions to the issue of a

Christian theology of religions in his stress on the value of a scientific study of, and living encounter with, non-Christian religions. He eschews any cultural prejudice and superiority. Furthermore, against Hick and other pluralists, he argues that the totalitarian nature of religion checks against the easy equation of surface similarities and points of contact. Furthermore, when, for example, Hick asserts that all religions are a quest for liberation from self-centredness to Reality-centredness, Kraemer's contention that the religions often address different questions and therefore may give different answers, must be kept in mind. He writes, for instance, of the missionary testimony in Africa, that 'not the consciousness of sin brings men to Christ, but the continued contact with Christ brings them to consciousness of sin'.[45] Or again, concerning the quest of the Advaitin mystic, Kraemer writes: 'At the end the only thing that appears to exist really in this whole mirage of existence is human consciousness moving in sovereign solitude over the void abyss of void existence.'[46] Kraemer contends that this goal is far removed from the Christian's desire for loving union with God. These very real and sometimes contradictory differences between the religions cannot be minimized or easily harmonized. In chapter 2 we saw how precisely such problems created obstacles to the acceptance of the pluralist position.

However, there are a number of critical questions that can be addressed to Kraemer; some of these are related to issues that will be developed later in this chapter. Two major criticisms of Kraemer's phenomenological reflections may be formulated thus: although his emphasis on the totalitarian nature of religion provides a salutary check against surface similarities and comparisons, does he not neglect the dynamic nature of religion as well as the creative interaction between beliefs and practice which result in the development and changes within religious traditions? A recognition of these latter features would, in principle, preclude any *final* judgement upon the religious life of humankind, and require a more nuanced analysis than Kraemer provides. Secondly, and connectedly, he seems to preclude some genuine points of contact and similarities because his theological assumption about the *sui generis* character of Christ's revelation forestalls a proper historical and hermeneutically sensitive analysis. Is a genuine openness to the possibility of God's action and presence in the non-

Christian religions really possible on Kraemer's Christological axioms?

Let me begin with the first objection. Surely Kraemer underestimates the dynamic and changing nature of religions because of his overemphasis on their totalitarian nature. In the previous chapter good grounds were offered for rejecting Smith's sharp distinction between faith and beliefs, and his perhaps too individualistic understanding of religion. On the other hand (and against Kraemer), it was acknowledged that because of the variety of beliefs within a single religion such as Hinduism, it is sometimes necessary to abandon umbrella terms like Hinduism and speak of Advaita Vedanta, Visistadvaita or Samkhya Yoga and so on. History, which is still in the making, may produce even further differences and modifications within 'Hinduism', as it has in fact already done. Too often, Kraemer seems to neglect this complexity, analysing and negatively evaluating, say, the Hindu theistic *bhakti* devotional traditions of Ramanuja and Kabir. (And what of the new theistic Hindu developments such as the Hare Krishna cult?)

Kraemer employs the questionable assumption that because these movements are part of Hinduism, they are 'fundamentally anthropocentric, as all good *monistic, mystic* Hindu religion is'.[47] Such a procedure is historically and phenomenologically reductive and limiting. Mariasusai Dhavamony, for instance, has concluded, after an exhaustive and sensitive analysis of the theistic Saiva Siddhanta literature, that, in Saiva Siddhanta, 'God is love: all his actions in the world are realized out of love for "creatures" and have the purpose of leading souls to loving union with him'.[48] It would be entirely improper to interpret this particular Hindu religious tradition in terms of anthropocentric monism. In the space of such a short study, I cannot pursue this point but refer the reader to a number of competent studies which certainly undermine Kraemer's overemphasis on the totalitarian nature of religions, especially with reference to his interpretation of the theistic and *bhakti* traditions within Hinduism.[49]

I do not intend to deny that there may be genuine and irreconcilable differences or astounding and significant similarities between the theistic *bhakti* traditions of India and Christ's revelation of a God of mercy, love, forgiveness and judgement.

But I do wish to object that Kraemer is often insensitive to these possibilities because of his Christologically exclusivist starting point and also his phenomenological method and assumptions. His insensitivity is evident when he dismisses the almost Lutheran insights of Shinran's Japanese Shin-Shu Amida, where the principle of faith in grace alone, as against effecting salvation by works, is strongly emphasized. Kraemer discards this phenomenon on the questionable grounds that Shin-Shu must be viewed in the light of the 'naturalistic monism [of] Mahayana Buddhism'.[50] There are, I believe, many points of contact and similarity which Kraemer obscures by his reductive hermeneutic.[51]

In addition, Kraemer does not pay enough attention to the way in which a religion's 'classical' doctrines and axioms begin to change in the light of practice. Again, the continual movement of history and the possible surprises it may bring cannot be minimized. For instance, Richard Gombrich has shown how classical Theravada Buddhism has undergone a quiet but radical change in the light of its practice in the village of Migala in Sri Lanka, especially in relation to the central notion of *karunavanta* (kindness/compassion).[52] Kraemer, for instance, argues that the notion of *ahimsa*, much popularized and praised because of the life and teachings of Gandhi, should be viewed in terms of its soteriological roots: 'The goal of individual deliverance from the suffering of existence engendered the meticulous desire to lessen the chances of re-birth by avoiding infliction of suffering, but in the long run it became, *psychologically* speaking, positive benevolence towards all beings.'[53]

By limiting his view of *ahimsa* to its historical soteriological roots alone, Kraemer tends to neglect the way in which the psychological component here can lead to a deeper rethinking and understanding, as is reflected in some strands of modern Hinduism. This is clearly the case with the notion of *karunavanta* in modern Buddhism, as is witnessed in the village of Migila. Such changes are also evident in Christianity, where for instance, the notion of 'salvation' is almost diametrically understood in some part of the Third World compared to more comfortable parts of the First.[54] This warning against an abstract and over-textual analysis of religions can also be directed at pluralists such as Hick and Race.

To summarize: I have been arguing that there are a number of significant points of contact and similarity between Christian and non-Christian insights which become evident in phenomenological analysis. These are important. I have also been arguing that a methodological approach which steers clear of Smith's over-individualistic view of religion and Kraemer's overemphasis on the monolithic and totalitarian nature of religion, allows for a more sensitive and open phenomenological analysis.[55] Furthermore, because of the dynamic nature of religions brought about through the interaction of practice and belief, it follows that one cannot say, *a priori*, that all religions, past and future, exhibit human-made structures of self-justification. Similarly, points of continuity and contact cannot be denied *a priori*, if one is genuinely open to history and subsequent investigations. But Kraemer does seem to assert a final evaluation of the non-Christian religions, and a somewhat negative one at that, which brings me back to my second objection and also to the issue of Christology.

Theological considerations

I pointed out in my exposition of Kraemer's thought, how he tries to bypass the unhistorical and *a priori* approach of Barth. If Kraemer's phenomenological openness is taken seriously, I have shown above that a final evaluation of the non-Christian religions, past, present and future, is impossible and unhistorical. Yet Kraemer offers just such an evaluation, and he does this as a result of his Christology.

Because of the alleged *sui generis* nature of Christ's revelation, Kraemer is forced to deny any points of contact or similarity. Thus, at times he is surely in danger of falling back into a Barthian position, which he seeks to avoid. Kraemer makes the pertinent point that phenomenological analysis cannot of itself provide truth criteria, but it is my contention that Kraemer's *exclusivist* Christological truth criterion is in serious conflict with his attempted phenomenological openness. I shall use this objection as a way of entering into further criticism of Kraemer's overemphasis on salvation through Christ alone, often at the cost of the axiom of the universal salvific will of God.

The whole weight of Kraemer's exclusivist approach rests on

his constant emphasis that 'God has revealed *the* Way and *the* Life and *the* Truth in Jesus Christ', and that in the light of this revelation '*all* [my emphasis] religious life, the lofty and degraded, appear to be under the divine judgement, because it is *misdirected*'.[56] From my conclusions in chapter 2, I would agree with Kraemer's point that Christian talk of God derives primarily from the revelation in Christ. But we may ask whether Kraemer's exclusivist Christology is the only viable alternative to the reductive Christologies offered by the pluralists. In what follows I shall argue that it is not (and will explore this point further in chapter 4). More significantly, I shall also argue that Kraemer and like-minded exclusivists have difficulties in maintaining the internal coherency of their exclusivist position.

We have seen how Kraemer admits that God is working outside the confines of the Christian revelation, in nature, history, conscience and through a universal religious consciousness. Permissibly, he contends, against pluralists, that this activity is only recognized in the light of Christ's revelation. But, at the same time, with difficulty, he contends that *all* religious life is misdirected in the light of the *sui generis* revelation of God in Christ.

Can he hold these assertions together? Already, we have had grounds for questioning Kraemer's overemphasis on the totalitarian nature of religions and his distorted and unhistorical judgement on all religious life. Now we may ask in what sense can Kraemer claim a *sui generis* status for the *event* of God's revelation in Christ, in the light of his own admission that God works outside of this revelation?

In fact a number of critics point out that Kraemer's Christology eventually forces him to deny any revelation outside Christ. However, in the light of Kraemer's explicit denial of this, I have adopted Kraemer's reading of his own work, although in what follows, we shall notice good grounds for these critics' disquiet.[57]

When Kraemer's *The Christian Message in a Non-Christian World* was published, one of his most astute critics focused upon this very issue. Alfred Hogg questioned Kraemer's thesis from a biblical standpoint, arguing that the Bible shows that God has revealed himself elsewhere, although often these revelations have been distorted or manipulated by sinful human beings.[58]

Hogg rightly went on to point out that if this much was admitted, then surely too much was admitted, for what then becomes of the allegedly *sui generis* character of the revelation in Christ? It is one thing to say that Christ is the normative criterion, but another to imply that by this criterion all other revelations, however distorted or manipulated, are to be denied. Hogg also argued that since God revealed himself in Christ to be a loving father of 'generous, unlimited Divine love', surely the Christian cannot but believe that God 'is *always* and everywhere seeking to reveal Himself to *every* man'.[59]

We can pursue these biblical and theological criticisms of Kraemer's exclusivist theology in the light of God's revelation in Israel's history. Israel's understanding, acceptance and faith in *Yahweh*, although faltering, provides a test case for examining the coherence of Kraemer's and other exclusivists' assertions that salvation is only possible through explicit confession and surrender to the revelation of God in Christ. If this exclusivist contention is taken seriously, then it must imply that the revelation of God in Israel's history was either (*a*) not revelation after all, or (*b*) a revelation, but somehow inadequate for salvation.[60]

Kraemer seems to disavow the first option, when he writes: 'The whole of the Old Testament from Genesis to Malachi is the record of *God's revelatory working* on the people of Israel.'[61] Clearly Christian exclusivists who flatly deny *any* revelation outside Jesus Christ would be hard-pressed to explain the use of the Old Testament as part of Christian scripture! The Old Testament stands as a solid testimony, accepted by nearly all Christians, of God's activity in history. The crucial point to be noted is that such a testimony clearly indicates that God's activity cannot be confined to the historical event of Jesus' life, death and resurrection. However, like Kraemer, most exclusivists adopt my option (*b*), that is, that there is revelation outside Christ, but that it is inadequate for salvation. But it is precisely at this point that the exclusivist position begins to show signs of internal strain.

First, if there is revelation outside Jesus Christ, then it cannot be claimed that Jesus is the only or *sui generis* event of revelation. This tendency falls prone to the unnecessary and unbiblical exclusivism so strongly and legitimately criticized by pluralists. However, in reaction, pluralists seem to abandon any normative status for Christ's revelation, with many consequent difficulties. A legitimate and internally consistent claim would be to argue for the special and normative status of the *contents* of the Christian revelation, but not for the *event* of the Christian revelation *per se*. I shall investigate this strategy in chapter 4. For the moment, I can only point to this unresolved tension within the exclusivist, and especially Kraemer's, position.

A second and most crucial problem follows on from the acceptance of revelation in Israel's history. How can it be maintained that the only way to salvation is explicit confession and surrender to God in Christ, if God has truly revealed Himself in Israel's history before the coming of Jesus Christ? Kraemer's 'answer' adopted by many exclusivists, points to Israel's rejection of Jesus. The Jews 'did not recognize God in Him, and rejected God's self-disclosure in Christ . . . In the light of such questions the mystery of iniquity, precisely in the "highest" expressions of the human mind, looms up.'[62]

Kraemer is right in highlighting 'the mystery of iniquity', an aspect too often neglected by pluralists. But is this a satisfactory answer to our question? What of the many pious Jews before the time of Jesus; those who did submit entirely to God's self-disclosure within Israel's history? What of Abraham and Moses and the many holy men and women of Israel listed so eloquently in the Letter to the Hebrews, chapter 11? Relatedly, we may ask, what of the countless of millions of non-Christians who lived before the time of Jesus, or the many millions who have lived after the time of Jesus who have never heard the Gospel, often through no fault of their own? This question may apply to those who have never heard the Gospel in a literal sense, such as some undiscovered Amazonian tribe. It may also apply to those who have had the Gospel preached to them but have not understood or appropriated it through no fault of their own. For example, in 1513, Martin de Encisco read a short history of the world, the coming of Christ and the institution of the papacy, often in Latin, to South American Indians! If the Indians did not convert to Christianity, their lands were seized as they were seen to be wilful idolaters.

Can we really accept that the God revealed in Christ, a loving father of 'generous, unlimited Divine love', has denied so many millions the means to salvation – through no fault of their own? This pluralist question must be taken seriously. It is difficult to see how Kraemer can answer this question positively without compromising his central axiom that salvation only comes through confession and surrender to God in Christ. On the other hand, it is difficult to see how a negative answer can be squared with the admission that God has revealed himself and has often been accepted in Israel's history. It is also difficult to see how a negative answer can be squared with the venerable Christian axiom of the universal salvific will of God.

Exclusivist theologians tend to adopt either one of two strategies to relieve this awkward tension within their position. The first, adopted by Kraemer and Newbigin, simply states that we cannot know how those who do not know Christ are saved and must leave this to 'the wise mercy of God' and the 'mysterious workings of God's Spirit'.[63] In one sense this is true. When we discuss the salvation of non-Christians, or Christians for that matter, we cannot confidently assert that this or that person is saved or not – ultimately all rests within 'the mysterious workings of God's Spirit'. However, this answer seems painfully inadequate in the light of the pressing questions before us and it is not clear, if we use our test case of Israel, why there are supposedly inadequate grounds for attempting to probe the issue further. Kraemer, Newbigin and others seem to want to relieve this exclusivist internal tension without paying the price in terms of the theological implications of their answer.

Another strategy to lessen this internal tension is to argue that after death the person who has never heard of Christ will confront him, and then have the chance to choose for or against God.[64] Although there is no *a priori* reason why this option should be discounted, Hick's comment about implausible 'epicycles' comes to mind. Paul Knitter loosely expresses his dissatisfaction with this answer in the following way: 'Such suggestions seem to be rather arbitrary devices, theological speculations for a dilemma that, perhaps, is more a problem for theologians than for God. Through the haze of theological speculations, a simple question takes shape: Why can there not be other saviours besides Jesus?'[65]

It would certainly seem that 'arbitrary devices' are being employed to relieve this tension in exclusivist theology. Furthermore, and in the light of the test case of Israel, Knitter's question about the possibility of salvation outside the historical revelation of Christ seems to be substantiated.

I would also add one further criticism. Does not this strategy trivialize and minimize the historical and social nature of men and women? Surely these exclusivist theologians neglect the historical nature of God's action and adopt an almost gnostic solution, sometimes evading the real difficulty before them: is it possible, in principle, that a religion other than Christianity can provide the means of salvation? It would seem that exclusivists are forced, by their overemphasis upon the theological axiom that salvation is only possible by confession and surrender to Christ, to neglect the dominant pluralist axiom of the universal salvific will of God and thereby pronounce an entirely negative judgement upon the non-Christian religions.

One further point is worth noting. Kraemer's stark emphasis on the *sui generis* nature of Christ's revelation assumes a deep and unbridgeable gulf between God's grace and fallen humanity. To use a scholastic distinction, there is in Kraemer's Christology a commonly shared exclusivist assumption that Jesus Christ is the *efficient cause* of salvation. That is, salvation is constituted and brought about by Christ who is the sole bridge across the gaping abyss between God's grace and fallen humankind's sinfulness. This is why confession and submission to Christ is required. This type of Christology is also the reason why Kraemer is in constant danger of reducing all events, other than the Christ event, to purely human achievements and failures, despite his protestations to the contrary. This is also why Kraemer argues against natural theology because, for him, sin rather than nature or reason is opposed to grace. Consequently, men's and women's rational powers are inadequate and unable, because of their radically fallen situation, to reach a belief in God.

We have seen other difficulties resulting from this over-sharp distinction, but one may further ask whether Kraemer's notion of 'religious consciousness' (or the '*sensus divinitatis*') does not in fact imply that the gulf between humankind and God is not as wide as he tends to assume. Kraemer agrees with Calvin: 'It is clear that *sensus divinitatis* comes from God, "God has laid it (*indit*) in man".'[66] If a person's ability to respond to revelation is not by means of reason or through any faculty possessed by that person, but by this initiative of God, however misused and misdirected, is not this basic orientation towards God a gift of grace? What else can it be called? And if it is, can such an absolute rift between grace and sinful nature be maintained? I shall explore this issue in greater depth in chapter 4.

To summarize: I have been arguing that Kraemer's exclusivist emphasis on the axiom that salvation is only possible through confession and surrender to Christ is problematic on biblical, theological and internal grounds. I have argued this without assuming a break in the normative ontological link between Jesus and God, which pluralists are prone to do. I have also tried to point to the heart of the exclusivist dilemma – if revelation outside Christ is denied, this seems questionable on biblical and theological grounds. If revelation outside Christ is accepted, as it is more often than not, it is difficult to maintain the following claims and some of their implications: first, *sui generis* status of Christ's revelation; second, that Israel's revelatory encounter with God before Christ must have been an entirely unsatisfactory means of salvation; third, that a loving God would seem to have denied many millions of non-Christians the means to salvation often through no fault of their own: and fourth, that there is an absolute rift between nature and grace; in effect, that salvation is *only* possible through confession and surrender to Christ.

As in chapter 2, I have tried to show that emphasis on only one of the two crucial axioms that determine a Christian theology of religions leads to major theological and phenomenological problems. In the next chapter I shall inquire whether the inclusivist paradigm can resolve some of these profound difficulties, while maintaining the strengths of the exclusivist and pluralist insights. For the moment, I shall pursue two more questions arising from Kraemer's presentation of the exclusivist paradigm in order to tease out further relevant issues for the formulation of a viable Christian theology of religions.

Truth criteria

Kraemer's emphasis that the starting point or norm for truth must be based on the self-disclosure of God in Christ is an important contribution to the debate. Kraemer suggests that a Christian who does not start from Christ presupposes 'that there is another ultimate standard than Christ, a so-called religious *a priori* by which even Christ, who upsets all human standards, is measured'.[67] We have seen how the adoption of non-Christological truth criteria to discern God's activity runs into difficulties in the previous chapter. Hick, for instance, veers towards a confusing agnosticism in employing the criterion of a turning away from 'self-centredness to Reality-centredness'. Race ends up with a form of relativism which he criticizes in Troeltsch. Knitter, as was also noted in the previous chapter, draws heavily on Jung. Knitter's truth criterion requires that the 'vision of life' offered by the different religions 'actually promotes the psychological welfare and the liberation of both individuals and societies'.[68] Only in a footnote does he acknowledge that what makes for 'good psychology' begs an 'extremely complex question . . . concerning what is the fulfillment and goal of human nature.'[69] His Jungian answer begs the question, for this statement immediately takes us back to Christology in determining, from a Christian standpoint, what such a phrase as the 'fulfillment and goal of human nature' implies. Kraemer's suggestion rightly calls into question the basis and authority of the employment of non-Christological truth criteria within the Christian tradition.

If we avoid Kraemer's excessively restrictive interpretation of the Christological criterion, however, we may be freed from his tendency to deny truth and God's self-disclosing activity outside the Christ event. Furthermore, this can be done while maintaining an openness to other religious truths with Christ and his Spirit as the normative and definitive criteria. No evaluation of the non-Christian religions is possible without some sort of evaluative criteria.

Kraemer's further contribution regarding truth criteria is his contention that Christ's revelation cannot be reduced to a set of intellectual propositions or ideas, turning historical revelation into a kind of 'prolonged gnosis'.[70] One cannot carry out evaluation solely by means of comparing intellectual expressions. Religious traditions cannot be reduced to sets of propositional statements. Rituals, worship, practices, sentiment, existential decision and many other factors form part of the complex fabric of religious commitment and religious truth. Concerning the Christological truth criterion, it is instructive to note that Kraemer also points out the 'rich variety of approach, expression and experience' in the New Testament: John's emphasis on love; the emphasis on fulfilment in the Letter to the Hebrews; on joy, hope and patience in the First

Letter of Peter; James's emphasis on action and Paul's on faith alone and the sinfulness of humankind.[71] It is precisely this plurality of insights *within* the Christian tradition which facilitates an expansive and open use of the Christological truth criterion. But unfortunately, it is precisely here that Kraemer seems to fall short of his own insights.

I shall develop the positive side of these comments later, but for the moment I wish to argue that Kraemer tends to absolutize only one aspect of Christ's revelation of God (concerning humankind's sinfulness), which is excessively Pauline. It would seem that he employs his Christological criterion in a rather reductive and almost intellectualist fashion. Time and time again Kraemer dismisses the value of non-Christian insights because they lack the consciousness of sin and the need for forgiveness.[72] M. M. Thomas has lucidly expressed an objection to Kraemer's somewhat rigid use of the Christological truth criterion. After indicating the findings of a number of New Testament scholars, he writes:

> It is possible to argue that consciousness of sin is not the only consciousness to which the Gospel is relevant . . . sin as 'alienation from God' and as 'the wrongness of existence', may have many forms, and if Jesus Christ is God's answer to man, it may not be right to start theology by totally rejecting spiritual questions raised outside the Old (and New) Testament categories as altogether irrelevant to the Gospel. Some of them may be. But others may not be, and many indeed bring to light new facets of the Christian truth. Challenging relevance to the existing patterns of understanding may therefore be a better way to maintain *openness to new truths in Christ* than the one that rejects all but the categories of sin and salvation.[73]

Thomas's pertinent and profound remarks highlight Kraemer's single-minded adherence to a very narrow and closed form of an either–or model for dealing with truth-claims. We saw that the pluralist insistence on a both–and model for assimilating truth-claims runs into considerable difficulties. Here, it is equally clear that Kraemer's narrow use of an either–or model faces different, although equally difficult, objections. The notion of complementary truths cannot be easily accommodated within Kraemer's position. In fact, it has been pointed out that on Kraemer's view 'a very great deal in the religious heritage of Christendom [such as mysticism] must also be written down as dangerous aberrations'.[74]

This narrow Christological understanding is also the reason why Kraemer neglects the fatherly love of God, as Hogg and Hick put it. Instead, he tends to exclusively emphasize obedience and submission to God in Christ. Furthermore, the quotation above from Thomas also highlights the value of a Christological criterion characterized by openness. Although Kraemer does say that the Christian can and should learn from the non-Christian, it is sometimes difficult to see how this is theologically possible on Kraemer's premises. However, against the pluralists, it must be pointed out that the normativeness of Christ's revelation will be determinative when a both–and model of assessing truth claims is required, unless conversion takes place and a new centre of perspective and balance is adopted. If someone is converted away from Christianity, then their determinative criterion will no longer be Christ.

Clearly, what is needed is a judicious use of both the either–or and the both–and models, whenever appropriate, rather than the *a priori* adoption of one rather than the other. In this way it seems possible to remain committed, while truly open to whatever riches are discovered in the lives and religions of non-Christians, both past, present and to come.

One further point is relevant to this discussion of truth criteria. Kraemer argues, perhaps too emphatically, against a tradition of pluralist pragmatism that value and truth should not be equated. There is, says Kraemer, a certain ambiguity in the notion of value because 'fictions and even lies have been extraordinarily valuable and successful', and furthermore, it is 'philosophically superficial to equate the psychic experience of satisfaction with the certainty that [the experience] is therefore true in the deepest sense, or is related to realities which are true'.[75] While all this cannot be denied (and reminds one of Hick's criticisms concerning Nazism and warlock worship against Smith's apparent adoption of pragmatist and non-cognitive views), surely value and truth cannot be totally prised apart? For instance, does not a true act of selfless love somehow partake in the reality of the selfless love of God disclosed in Jesus? In Matthew 25:31–46 (the last judgement scene where the righteous ask, 'Lord, when did we see thee hungry and feed thee, or thirsty and give thee drink?'), it seems that the righteous, gathered from 'all the nations', are chosen because unknown to them, when they exercised true compassion and mercy (Matthew 9:13; 12:7), they also thereby loved the Lord (Matthew 18:5). Although we cannot wrench this passage from its context and minimize hermeneutical difficulties, it certainly makes the telling point, that this and other passages indicate that radical selfless love of another also involves love of God.[76] Therefore, against Kraemer, the question of religious truth is surely connected with the question of action and value; although, with Kraemer, we should beware of reducing the question of truth to action alone, as is the tendency of Knitter.

The place of Christianity

Before concluding this chapter, it is worth indicating a rather discordant note in Kraemer's appraisal of the difference between empirical Christianity and the revelation of Christ, under which the former is judged. This point is worth pursuing because it both reflects Kraemer's very Barthian outlook and is shared by a number of exclusivists. Also, Hick directs his criticism at those who put either Christ or Christianity at the centre. However, we may now question whether the two can be entirely separated.

Some of the most penetrating criticisms of Kraemer's absolute distinction between empirical Christianity and the revelation of Christ come from his fellow exclusivist, Lesslie Newbigin. Newbigin criticizes Kraemer on the grounds that the truth of the Gospel cannot be spoken of in abstraction from the communities' traditions which communicate it. In some respects this follows from the totalitarian nature of religion and from the basic fact that the Bible, itself, is nothing other than the testimony and witness of the early Christian communities. To put this in another way: there can be no revelation without the experiencer expressing, remembering and transmitting it. Revelation takes place within a social and historical context.[77] This is why Newbigin writes, rightly in my opinion: 'The claim that . . . Christ is decisive for all human life is a meaningless claim except as it is interpreted in the life of the community which lives by the tradition of the apostolic testimony. There cannot, therefore, be a *total* disjunction between the Gospel and "Christianity".'[78] Kraemer is certainly right that the two cannot be identified, but he seems to prise apart too strongly that which must be held closer together.[79]

CONCLUSION

Through this detailed investigation of a major and influential exclusivist, I have tried to isolate certain theological and phenomenological assumptions common to the exclusivist paradigm. This view certainly has a number of strengths, often in contrast to pluralist weaknesses. Conversely, its major weaknesses are often reflected in pluralist strengths. Exclusivists, while correctly stressing that salvation comes from God alone through Christ, sometimes fail to develop one of the major insights resulting from this revelation – that of the universal salvific will of God. The latter axiom is strongly emphasized by pluralists. Exclusivists rightly stress the normativeness of Christ in evaluating different religious truth-claims, as opposed to criteria often imported from outside this norm by pluralists. However, for some exclusivists, this criterion is used in a narrow and restrictive fashion, tending unnecessarily to limit the revelatory activity of God to the Christ event. Exclusivists consequently tend to adopt an either–or model of truth, compared to the both–and model of pluralists. However, the tendency to use either one of these models alone leads to irresolvable difficulties. Therefore, while pluralists too often indiscriminately assume the salvific nature of non-Christian religions, the exclusivists, when they do acknowledge revelation outside Christianity, either deny it any salvific efficacy or tend to minimize the implications of this admission. Finally, while in principle many exclusivists can and do avoid the pluralist charges of superiority and chauvinism in dialogue, it sometimes appears that as a result of their theological axioms there is little place for mutual enrichment. However, practical cooperation and moral tolerance is an imperative for most exclusivists. Furthermore, complementing pluralist shortcomings, mission, service and worship are seen by many exclusivists as intrinsically and indissolubly related.

If we have reason to be dissatisfied with certain aspects of the pluralist and exclusivist paradigms, while rightly admiring other features, we may now turn to the inclusivist position, exemplified in the thought of Karl Rahner, to further the dialogue and pursue these complicated issues, tentatively moving towards a viable Christian theology of religions.

NOTES

1. R. Slater, 'Christian attitudes to other religions', *Canadian Journal of Theology*, 2 (1956), p. 217.
2. Kraemer, *Christian Message*, p. ix.
3. For surveys see Race, *Christians and Religious Pluralism*, ch. 2; Knitter, *No Other Name?*, ch. 5, 6.
4. Kraemer, *Christian Message*, p. v.
5. *Tambaram-Madras Series: International Missionary Council Meeting*, vol. 1 (1939), p. 10.
6. Kraemer, *Christian Message*, p. 107.
7. See Kraemer, *Religion and the Christian Faith* (1956), pp. 23ff, 31ff. I am in agreement with this assessment, as are a number of scholars such as C. Davis, *Christ and the World Religions* (1970), p. 47; M. Braybrooke, *Together to the Truth: Developments in Hindu and Christian Thought since 1800* (1971), pp. 119–20.
8. For accounts of Kraemer's life, see Hallencreutz, *From Kraemer Towards Tambaram*; Jathanna, *The Decisiveness of the Christ-Event*, pp. 62–70; A. Th. van Leeuwen, *Hendrik Kraemer: Dienaar der Wereldkerke* (1959).
9. D. Niles, 'Karl Barth – A personal memory', *The South East Asian Journal of Theology*, 11 (1969), pp. 10–11. Kraemer's position is therefore misleadingly and polemically characterized by H. D. Lewis, *Jesus in the Faith of Christians* (1981), p. 96.
10. Kraemer, *Christian Message*, p. 109.
11. Kraemer, *Religion*, p. 66.
12. Kraemer, *Christian Message*, p. 108. Also see, for example, K. Barth, *Church Dogmatics*, vol. 1/2 (1956), pp. 299ff; E. Brunner, 'Revelation and religion', in O. Thomas (ed.), *Attitudes Towards Other Religions* (1969), pp. 122ff.
13. See, for example, the work of B. Kristen, *The Meaning of Religion: Lectures in the Phenomenology of Religion* (1960), with an introduction by Kraemer. Kraemer's term 'totalitarian' should not be associated with its more recent political usage.
14. Hick, *Second Christianity*, p. 86; Knitter, *No Other Name?*, p. 118.
15. Kraemer, *Christian Message*, p. 135.
16. Ibid., pp. 138–9.
17. Kraemer, *Religion*, p. 51.

18. Kraemer, *Why Christianity of All Religions?* (1962), p. 15. See also Barth, *Church Dogmatics*, vol. 1/2, p. 301; Brunner, 'Revelation and religion', pp. 122ff; L. Newbigin, *The Open Secret* (1978), pp. 73ff.
19. Kraemer, *Christian Message*, p. 101.
20. Ibid., p. 107.
21. Ibid., p. 432.
22. Ibid., p. 303.
23. Ibid., p. 432.
24. Ibid., pp. 47ff, 59–60, 432.
25. Kraemer, *Why Christianity?*, p. 121, quoting K. Mannheim.
26. Ibid., p. 123. Unfortunately, Kraemer does not give many examples.
27. See Barth, *Church Dogmatics*, vols 4/3 (1962), pp. 773, 872–6; P. Beyerhaus, 'Mission and humanization', *International Review of Missions*, 60 (1971), p. 21.
28. Kraemer, *Christian Message*, pp. 75–6; *Religion*, part 4.
29. Also see Barth, *Church Dogmatics*, vols 1/2, pp. 299ff; Brunner, 'Revelation and religion', p. 131; W. Pannenberg, *Basic Questions in Theology*, vol. 2 (1971), p. 114.
30. Kraemer, *Why Christianity?*, p. 114.
31. Kraemer, *Christian Message*, p. 74. Kraemer clearly stands in the Reformation tradition.
32. Kraemer, *Religion*, p. 334 (my italics).
33. Kraemer, *Christian Message*, ch. 5, 6, 7.
34. Kraemer, 'Continuity or discontinuity' in W. Paton (ed.), *The Authority of Faith* (1939), p. 21; *Religion*, ch. 20 deals with the topic of general revelation and its history.
35. Kraemer, *Christian Message*, p. 136.
36. Ibid., p. 122.
37. Barth was possibly more dialectical in the light of his later works; see D. Baillie and H. Martin (eds), *Revelation* (1937), pp. 79–80; Barth, *Church Dogmatics*, vol. 4, pp. 575ff. For recent examples of this clearly undialectical evaluation, see the Frankfurt Declaration, *Christianity Today*, 14 (1970), pp. 844–6 and the Lausanne Declaration, *How Shall They Hear? Proceedings and Reports from the Consultation of World Evangelization* (1981); and H. Lindsell, 'Missionary imperative: A conservative evangelical exposition', in N. Horner (ed.), *Protestant Currents in Mission: The Ecumenical–Conservative Encounter* (1968).
38. Kraemer, *Christian Message*, p. 113.
39. Kraemer, *Religion*, p. 232.
40. Kraemer, *Christian Message*, p. 120.
41. Ibid., p. 125; *Religion*, ch. 20.
42. Kraemer, *Religion*, p. 171.

43. Kraemer, *Christian Message*, p. 112.
44. Ibid., pp. 126–7.
45. Ibid., p. 345.
46. Ibid., pp. 166–7.
47. Ibid., p. 171 (my italics).
48. M. Dhavomony, *Love of God According to Saiva Siddhanta* (1971), p. 378.
49. See R. Zaehner, *At Sundry Times* (1958), ch. 2, 3, and his *The Concordant Discord* (1970), ch. 6–8; A. J. Appasamy, *The Gospel and India's Heritage* (1942); R. Otto, *India's Religion of Grace and Christianity Compared and Contrasted* (1930); J. Carpenter, *Theism in Medieval India* (1921); S. Kulandran, *Grace: A Comparative Study of the Doctrine in Christianity and Hinduism* (1964).
50. Kraemer, *Christian Message*, p. 181.
51. Regarding Buddhism, see, for example, R. H. Drummond, *Gautama the Buddha: An Essay in Religious Understanding* (1974); H. Doumlin, *Christianity Meets Buddhism* (1974); A. Graham, *Zen Catholicism: A Suggestion* (1963).
52. R. Gombrich, *Precept and Practice* (1971), and also my discussion of this topic in 'Elephants, ropes and a theology of religions'.
53. Kraemer, *Christian Message*, p. 165 (my italics).
54. See, for example, G. Gutierrez, *A Theology of Liberation: History, Politics and Salvation* (1974), ch. 9, and for an opposite view, E. R. Norman, *Christianity and the World Order* (1979).
55. See, for instance, N. Smart, *The Religious Experience of Mankind* (1977) ch. 1, and *The Phenomenon of Religion* (1978); Hick, *World's Religious Traditions*, pp. 379–91.
56. Kraemer, *Christian Message*, p. 136 (author's emphasis except where indicated).
57. See Kraemer's explicit denial of such interpretations (*Religion*, p. 232) found, for instance, in the views of A. Hogg and H. Farmer in W. Paton (ed.), *The Authority of Faith*, pp. 108, 158, 171; E. Sharpe, *Faith Meets Faith: Some Christian Attitudes to Hinduism in the Nineteenth and Twentieth Centuries* (1977), p. 96; Newbigin, *Finality of Christ*, pp. 36–8, thinks that Kraemer never squarely faces this issue, hence the problems that have caused such criticisms.
58. See, for instance: Wisdom of Solomon 13:1,6; Romans 1:18ff, 2:12–16; Acts 14:15ff, 17:22ff; John 1; Hebrews 1:1. K. Cracknell, *Towards a New Relationship: Christians and People of Other Faiths* (1986) deals with the positive, and also the more difficult and controversial biblical passages concerning God's activity outside Israel and Christianity, arguing that the biblical evidence runs contrary to an exclusivist reading. My thanks to Kenneth Cracknell for letting me see his manuscript before publication.

59. Kraemer, *Authority*, p. 102, and Hogg's *Towards Clarifying My Reactions to Doctor Kraemer's Book* (1938).
60. Knitter, *No Other Name?*, ch. 6, lists and points out many ('liberal') exclusivists who accept the occurrence of revelation outside Christ, but then argue that it is not adequate for salvation.
61. Kraemer, *Christian Message*, p. 227 (my italics).
62. Kraemer, *Religion*, p. 227; *Christian Message*, pp. 226ff.
63. L. Newbigin, 'The basis, purpose and manner of inter-faith dialogue', in R. Rousseau (ed.), *Interreligious Dialogue* (1981), p. 20; Kraemer, *Authority*, p. 4.
64. Lindbeck, *The Nature of Doctrine*, pp. 59ff; C. Braaten, *The Flaming Center: A Theology of the Christian Mission* (1977), p. 117; L. Boros, *The Moment of Truth* (1965); see also note 23 to my chapter 1.
65. Knitter, *No Other Name?*, p. 117.
66. Kraemer, *Religion*, p. 171.
67. Kraemer, *Authority*, p. 9.
68. Knitter, *No Other Name?*, p. 269.
69. Ibid., p. 240.
70. Kraemer, *Christian Message*, p. 71.
71. Ibid., p. 84.
72. Ibid., ch. 5–7; *Religion*, ch. 10, 12, 17; *Why Christianity?*, pp. 61ff.
73. M. Thomas, *The Acknowledged Christ of the Indian Renaissance* (1969), pp. 304–5 (my italics).
74. S. George, *Gandhi's Challenge to Christianity* (1939), p. 65 (my comment in parentheses). George cites the example of mysticism earlier in the text.
75. Kraemer, *Religion*, p. 85.
76. See also James 2:14–26; Matthew 7:15–21; Luke 6:43–9. See Karl Rahner's illuminating comments on pertinent scriptural passages in *Theological Investigations*, vol. 6 (1969), ch. 16, esp. pp. 234ff.
77. See D. Tracy's *The Analogical Imagination* (1981), ch. 5, 9, 10.
78. Newbigin, *Finality of Christ*, p. 77.
79. However, K. Cragg points out that in Kraemer's later works there seemed to be a shift 'away from the issue of truth in theology towards the obligation of truth in community', thereby taking greater account of the Church as mediator of the Gospel: see *The Christian and Other Religions* (1977), p. 7.

CHAPTER 4

The Inclusivist Paradigm

In this chapter I shall examine the inclusivist approach to other religions. This approach has been characterized as one that affirms the salvific presence of God in non-Christian religions while still maintaining that Christ is the definitive and authoritative revelation of God. Although we found reasons to be dissatisfied with the pluralist and exclusivist approaches, theologians from both these positions have levelled searching and serious criticisms against the inclusivist paradigm. Can inclusivists overcome these objections?

In the previous chapter I created a dialogue between pluralists and exclusivists. Now, all three partners will be summoned; hence the structure of this chapter will be somewhat different from the previous two, so as to facilitate this challenging and critical dialogue. After outlining Karl Rahner's version of inclusivism, I shall then deal with objections posed by exclusivists and pluralists. Hence, I shall be examining the inclusivist paradigm in some depth and revisiting issues raised in the previous two chapters.

Inclusivism is by no means a modern Roman Catholic phenomenon.[1] We have seen how its twentieth century roots go back to the Protestant missionary John Farquhar. However, it has been noted that since Vatican II, a large number of Catholic theologians have taken this inclusivist stance.[2] It has also been rightly noticed that if 'Vatican II is a watershed in Christian attitudes towards other religions, Karl Rahner is its chief engineer', and that 'the major architect of the post-conciliar Catholic contribution to the subject is undoubtedly Karl Rahner'.[3] Let us therefore examine this theologian whose theological enterprise has been compared to that of Plotinus, Augustine, Anselm and Bonaventure.[4]

KARL RAHNER'S INCLUSIVISM

Karl Rahner was born on 4 March 1904 in Freiburg im Breisgau, Germany. At the age of 18 he entered the Society of Jesus, and after ten years of intensive study, in 1932 he was ordained a Jesuit priest. He then began his doctoral studies on Thomas Aquinas's epistemology and spent some time in Freiburg attending Martin Heidegger's seminars on Kant. In his doctorate, which was to be later published as *Spirit in the World* in 1939, Rahner argued for the possibility of a post-Kantian metaphysics. As his ideas in this early book are crucial for an understanding of Rahner's entire theology, I shall briefly explain his central notion of *Vorgriff*, or what he also calls the 'supernatural existential'. (Rahner's German background and terminology often create difficulties for Anglo-Saxon readers.)

Rahner begins by examining our ability to know and differentiate between specific and historical particulars. This faculty and type of knowledge he calls 'categorial' knowledge; the ability to grasp and know the particularities of historical experience. Rahner argued that the very possibility of the intellect differentiating between things, the possibility of specific knowledge, requires and implies that we have a pre-apprehension of an infinite range of possibilities, of infinite being, which is fullness rather than void. To know that what I am writing with is a pen and not any other thing, implies (hence the term 'pre-apprehension') that my act of knowing is also related to the possibility of unlimited being. In effect, nothing need be as it is; thus everything we grasp, we understand as one possible limitation or determination of an infinite range of possibilities.[5]

From a Christian standpoint, Rahner maintains that this fundamental implicit communion with unlimited being in the act of knowing is a basic openness in a person's nature to the mystery of being, which is God. Hence, there is a pre-reflective, pre-apprehension of God inbuilt into our very nature – which Rahner calls 'transcendental revelation'. Consequently, he maintains that every time we reach beyond ourselves – for instance in acts of selfless love, in the experience of deep beauty, by following what is true and good whatever the cost, or in acts of trust and hope – we are experiencing and responding to grace mediated through the categorial, whether or not this is recognized. In this respect, if a person totally gives of themself in trust and love to another, they are only able to do this by grace. In positively responding to grace, they implicitly accept the mystery of being – which the Christian calls God.

This transcendental orientation of persons provides a basis for the question whether this mystery (a real but unknown 'God') has acted or spoken in the world, in history. Rahner maintains that his whole understanding of the nature of God and persons is only clarified and made possible through the historical and categorial revelation in Jesus. In the life, death and resurrection of Jesus the mystery of being, which is present to all persons by virtue of their nature, discloses itself and makes itself known as absolute self-giving and total love. Hence, anthropology, Christology and revelation are inseparable. Consequently, Rahner writes that 'Christology may be studied as self-transcending anthropology, and anthropology as deficient Christology'.[6] All questions about God and human beings can only be answered with reference to Jesus. I shall return to these themes later.

After his doctoral studies, Rahner became Professor of Theology at the Jesuit faculty at Innsbruck in 1938. Here be began to collect his theological reflections together in what eventually, over years of writing, extended to 20 volumes of *Theological Investigations*. At the time of his death, Rahner's list of publications ran into more than 3,000 items! The *Theological Investigations* contain his main contributions to the inclusivist paradigm, most clearly expressed in volume 5, in an essay entitled 'Christianity and non-Christian Religions'. Between 1939 and 1944, after the Nazis closed down the Innsbruck faculty and banished Rahner, he devoted himself to pastoral work and lecturing in Vienna. Through this experience, Rahner became well acquainted with many pastoral problems, especially those brought on by technology and secularization. Although he returned to Germany in 1945 as Professor of Theology in Pullach, and later held Professorships at the Universities of Innsbruck, Munich and Munster (where he died in 1984), Rahner's theological reflections are characterized by a pastoral concern with the problems faced by Christians in the modern world.

During the 1960s he advised the German bishops at the

Second Vatican Council and, as has been noted, influenced many of the Council's deliberations. Ironically, before the Council Rahner's work had been much frowned upon. However, after the Council, Rahner became increasingly identified as a major spokesman for modern Catholic theology.

Unlike Kraemer and to a lesser extent Hick, Rahner was not closely acquainted with non-Christian religions. But like both men, he attempted to reflect on the vexing problem of the relationship between Christianity and the non-Christian religions as a committed and pastorally sensitive Christian.

Theological considerations

Rahner makes it clear that his starting point for reflecting on the non-Christian religions is 'out of the self-understanding of Christianity itself', not as a phenomenologist or orientalist but as a dogmatic and systematic theologian.[7] Rahner argues that this starting point involves the difficult and exciting task of holding together, and making sense of, the two axioms that determine the different approaches to the non-Christian religions. While wholeheartedly accepting the pluralist plea that an all-loving God could not have consigned the majority of humankind to perdition, Rahner maintains, with the exclusivists, that salvation comes only through faith in God through Christ. It should be further noted that for Rahner this latter axiom is understood ecclesiologically; salvation comes only through the grace of God in Christ mediated in his Church. He sees the problem thus:

> When we have to keep in mind both principles together, namely the necessity of Christian faith and the universal salvific will of God's love and omnipotence, we can only reconcile them by saying that somehow all men must be capable of being members of the Church; and this capacity must not be understood merely in the sense of an abstract and purely logical possibility, but as a real and historically concrete one.[8]

How does Rahner hold together these seemingly contradictory, yet important axioms? He proposes four essential theses, arguing that it is perfectly possible that God is savingly present *through* and not *despite* the non-Christian religions.

This consideration is demanded if we fully accept the universal salvific will of God, and is demonstrated in the test case of Israel's religion. But this recognition, he argues, does not compromise the claims of Christianity, for the presence of God in these non-Christian religions is the presence of Christ. Consequently, the grace-filled elements and salvific structures in the lives and religions of non-Christians find their final and proper fulfilment and completion in Christianity. Let us look in more detail at the steps of his argument and draw out the nuances of his inclusivist thesis.

First thesis   The first thesis is similar to Kraemer's, except that for Rahner, Christianity and not only Christ is affirmed: 'Christianity understands itself as the absolute religion, intended for all men, which cannot recognize any other religion besides itself as of equal right.'[9]

Rahner avoids Kraemer's minimization of the community of Christians which lives by, preserves, interprets and preaches the saving presence of God made known in Jesus. This community of Christians is founded and authorized by Jesus and visibly maintains and proclaims his presence through the power of the Spirit. This is one of the reasons why the Church is sometimes called the body of Christ.

At this point, Rahner adds a crucial qualification to the first thesis which significantly distinguishes his position from that of Kraemer. The fact that Christianity understands itself as the absolute religion and demands adherence, must be balanced by the difficulties involved in discerning 'when the existentially real demand is made by the absolute religion in its historically tangible form'.[10] In saying this, Rahner shows considerable sensitivity to the fact that the Christian Gospel has not reached all people, and its universal validity and demand cannot be seen in isolation from this historical and existential situation. This qualification involves two categories of people, as we saw in chapter 3: those who lived before New Testament times and those who lived and live after New Testament times but have never really encountered the Gospel, through no fault of their own. This sensitivity to historical and existential factors is shared and developed by a number of inclusivist theologians. It avoids the difficult exclusivist claim that all religions are rendered invalid at the moment of the incarnation.[11]

Second thesis   The second thesis follows on from the first. It is theologically based upon the universal salvific will of God (similar to pluralists), revealed in Christ (different from pluralists), and is historically exemplified in the religion of Israel. It is worth quoting Rahner's careful wording of his second thesis:

> Until the moment when the Gospel really enters into the historical situation of an individual, a non-Christian religion (even outside the Mosaic religion) does not merely contain elements of a natural knowledge of God, elements, moreover mixed up with human depravity which is the result of original sin and later aberrations. It contains also supernatural elements arising out of the grace which is given to men as a gratuitous gift on account of Christ. For this reason, a non-Christian religion can be recognized as a *lawful* religion (although only in different degrees) without thereby denying the error and depravity contained in it.[12]

Let us unravel the theological and historical considerations contained in this thesis. Rahner takes the theological axiom of God's universal salvific will revealed in Christ absolutely seriously. Although it does not imply any certainty about a particular individual's salvation, he argues that it does mean that God must somehow offer grace to all those who have never properly encountered the Gospel. If the Christian revelation is to mean anything, then this much is certain. But if there is an offer of grace, is it mediated *through* or *despite* the non-Christian's religion? Rahner's answer is that it must be mediated through the non-Christian's religion, and like many pluralists, thinks that death-bed illuminations and private revelations are 'arbitrary and improbable postulates'.[13] More significantly, he argues that this type of exclusivist manoeuvre requiring death-bed or post-mortem experiences actually contradicts the character of the Christian revelation about the nature of persons because 'even in his most personal history man always remains a *social being*, whose innermost decisions are mediated through the specific form of his social and historical life'.[14] In fact, the very necessity of the first thesis would be questioned if the social and historical nature of men and women were denied. Therefore, Rahner argues that grace must be made available through and not despite the non-

Christian's religion, if it is made available at all. In this sense, non-Christian religions may be called 'lawful' when they mediate God's grace.

However, Rahner goes on to qualify this recognition in two ways. He is not unaware of 'human depravity' and 'original sin', which Kraemer and other exclusivists so emphatically identify in all human endeavour. These aberrations manifest themselves both in theory and in practice on the religious, ethical and metaphysical plane and are not to be treated as harmless or insignificant.[15] Despite this, Rahner argues that the Gospel does not justify a totally pessimistic view of men and women and, more positively, it does justify optimism in God's 'salvific will which is more powerful than the extremely limited stupidity and evil-mindedness of men'.[16] Furthermore, it is possible to envisage a religion which has both theoretical and practical errors which may nevertheless be deemed 'lawful'. In order to substantiate his case, Rahner carries out a theological analysis of the structure of the Old Covenant. (This was also the strategic test case employed in criticizing Kraemer in the previous chapter.)

Drawing on the history of Israel, Rahner shows that in the light of the New Testament there are many elements within Israel's religion which were willed by God *and* many elements which were false and corrupt. For instance, the preaching of the prophets testifies to both these aspects. The prophets constantly called Israel back to God's covenant while simultaneously pointing to corrupt and evil elements – both institutional and personal.[17] Rahner notes that despite these latter traces of corruption and depravity, the Old Covenant has always been recognized as 'lawful', until the time of the Gospel. According to many Christians, the Old Covenant was then grafted on to and fulfilled with the advent of the New Covenant. This view has been widely accepted in Christian history. The important point to note is that the Old Covenant facilitated and provided the concrete means by which many attained salvation. Rahner then suggests that these theological considerations may be applied, at least in principle, to other non-Christian religions. It is possible that other religions, despite error and corruption, may mediate grace which provides the means for salvation. Rahner clearly recognizes that there will be different degrees of error and truth found in the various non-Christian religions. It is the task of the

Christian phenomenologist to identify and analyse the non-Christian religions with these theological principles in mind.

Rahner's nuanced approach disavows a straight-forward either–or option between pluralism and exclusivism: 'We must . . . rid ourselves of the prejudice that we can face a non-Christian religion with the dilemma that it must either come from God in everything it contains, or be simply a human construction.'[18] These considerations, needless to say, also bear upon Christianity. Rahner freely acknowledges that sin, corruption and depravity are to be found within Christianity's long and chequered history. There should be no attempt to white-wash Christianity's past or present record. Matthew 13:19–30 makes it clear that a community that gives growth to weeds does not mean it cannot also give rise to wheat!

Rahner's second thesis must be understood in the light of these careful qualifications if it is to be properly appreciated. It should not be inferred that he thereby declares all non-Christian religions to be lawful, but only that in principle this is perfectly possible. He points to the theological considerations that determine this question and suggests that the Christian may be optimistic about the outcome.

Third thesis Rahner's third thesis follows on from the second and concerns mission. In the course of mission, when a Christian meets a non-Christian, the non-Christian cannot simply be regarded as a person deprived of salvific grace, living in a totally sinful and depraved condition, untouched in any way by God's grace and truth. From the reflections above, it is clear that a non-Christian may have already accepted God's grace in the depths of his or her heart, and it is for this reason that Rahner says they may be regarded as 'anonymous Christians'. If a non-Christian has responded positively to God's grace, for example, through selfless love for another, then, even though it is not known objectively, that person has accepted the God that is historically and definitively revealed in Christ. God's salvation cannot be divorced from Christ, hence the term 'anonymous Christian' is more appropriate than 'anonymous theist'. Talk of God's presence cannot be divorced from Christ's presence, as pluralists so often do. In propounding this form of the fulfilment theory, Rahner cuts across the assumptions of exclusivists like Barth and Kraemer.

Nevertheless, Rahner still argues that mission is absolutely necessary. The proclamation of the Gospel turns an anonymous Christian 'into someone who also knows about his Christian belief in the depths of his grace-endowed being by objective reflection and in the profession of faith which is given social form in the Church'.[19] It is Rahner's contention that because of a person's transcendental orientation (their 'hunger for God'), they will always be looking towards history to find the revelation of the mystery of being, which the Christian calls God. This event, according to Rahner, finds its definitive social and historical expression in Christ and his Church. Hence, the life of grace of the non-Christian finds its proper fulfilment and completion in the community of Christians, for grace is mediated in community and through history.

In this community, the grace to which Christians respond is proclaimed and sacramentally present. This is why Rahner writes that the 'incarnational and social structure of grace and Christianity', by its very nature, demands mission.[20] When a person explicitly and clearly grasps Christianity they enter a community committed to shaping their lives, whatever their own shortcomings and failures, in the light of God's definitive self-disclosure in the person of Christ. It is not simply a matter of making explicit what was only implicit before, but being transformed, moulded and nourished by the social and historical particulars of the liturgy, worship and sacramental structures of the Church. Rahner expresses this matter quite starkly when he writes that an individual who explicitly and clearly grasps Christianity, has 'other things being equal, a still greater chance of salvation than someone who is merely an anonymous Christian'.[21] The reverse side of this affirmation is the greater responsibility that consequently befalls a Christian, as he or she becomes clearly aware of the radical demands of the Gospel.

Fourth thesis   The fourth and final thesis concerns the Church. If the consequences of the previous theses are accepted, the Church cannot be seen as an elite community of those who are saved as opposed to the mass of unredeemed non-Christian humanity. The Church should instead be regarded as the 'historically tangible vanguard and the historically and socially constituted explicit expression of what the Christian hopes is present as a hidden reality even outside the visible Church'.[22] The Church is a tangible sign of the faith, hope and love made visible, present and irreversible in Christ. Rahner avoids the so-called logical chain of inference (according to critics like Hick), which leads to the notion that salvation is only possible for Christians as God is the founder of the Christian religion. Here again, he cuts across assumptions made by theologians examined in the previous chapters. This final thesis confirms that another view of the role and status of the Christian community is possible.

RAHNER'S INCLUSIVISM EVALUATED

Rahner's notion of the anonymous Christian has drawn much criticism from exclusivists and pluralists alike – and also from some inclusivists. By examining these criticisms we may now pursue questions concerning the viability of this attractive paradigm which tries to hold together the two crucial axioms which are so important to our question.

Dialogue and the idea of an anonymous Christian

John Hick, among others, has criticized the use of the term anonymous Christian for two reasons. Both concern the issue of dialogue. First, Hick argues that the concept of the anonymous Christian is *offensive* to non-Christians, reflecting a chauvinism and paternalism that creates barriers against open and trusting dialogue. It is 'an honorary status granted unilaterally to people who have not expressed any desire for it'.[23] Secondly, it creates a *stalemate* in dialogue, for 'it is as easy, and as arbitrary, to label devout Christians as anonymous Muslims, or anonymous Hindus, as to label devout Hindus or Muslims as anonymous Christians'.[24]

I wish to argue that these criticisms misunderstand the context of Rahner's reflections. He clearly states that his considerations form part of an internal, Christian reflection on the relation of Christianity to other religions. Consequently, the reflection is not addressed to, or meant to gain approval from, Hindus, Buddhists and others. It is addressed by a Christian to his or her, and the Church's, own self-understanding. An analogy will demonstrate my point. If a Buddhist or Muslim questioned or disagreed with a Christian's understanding of the incarnation, Trinity and grace, this would surely be insufficient reason to abandon the meaning that is properly intended by these terms. I do not wish to imply that the questions and difficulties posed by such non-Christians be ignored, or that a Christian should be insensitive to the thought-forms and cultures of non-Christians when expressing Christian insights. I simply want to indicate the proper context within which Rahner formulates his theory, consequently rendering these charges invalid. It would be perfectly possible to abandon the *term* 'anonymous Christian' but not the underlying conviction and reality which it denotes – that when a person is saved, it is by God's grace that they are saved.

In fact, I would argue that the notion of an anonymous Christian actually facilitates rather than obstructs dialogue for it designates the possibility of grace in the dialogue partner's life and religion. Therefore, it avoids the *a priori* Barthian exclusivism which characterizes the partner's life and religion as erroneous; and the reductive forms of pluralism which neglect real differences between dialogue partners. Furthermore, it provides good theological grounds for the pluralist affirmation, which is never properly substantiated (and surely as paternalistic), that God is at work in the non-Christian religions. Consequently, the inclusivist may engage in dialogue with a truly respectful, attentive and critical attitude, knowing that God may already be present in the partner's life and religion.

What of Hick's further objection concerning the reversal of labels? What if a Zen Buddhist called a Christian an anonymous Zen Buddhist? Hick argues that this inclusivist strategy perpetuates a stalemate in dialogue. It is worth recounting a conversation of Rahner's with Keji Nishitani, the Japanese philosopher and head of the Kyoto Zen Buddhist school. Nishitani asked Rahner how he would respond if treated as an anonymous Zen Buddhist. Rahner replied:

> Certainly you may and should do so from your point of view; I feel myself honoured by such an interpretation, even if I am obliged to regard you as being in error or if I assume that, correctly understood, to be a genuine Zen Buddhist is identical with being a genuine Christian, in the sense directly and properly intended

by such statements. Of course in terms of objective social awareness it is indeed clear that the Buddhist is not a Christian and the Christian is not a Buddhist. Nishitani replied: Then on this point we are entirely at one.[25]

There are a number of important points worth noting in Rahner's answer. First, the internal logic of a non-Christian's belief may lead to this type of reverse designation. This is both permissible and understandable. It need not be the cause of scandal or stalemate. (Rahner even says that he was 'honoured' by such a designation!) The main point that Rahner is striving to state is the conviction that grace may, and quite rightly can, be operative in the Zen Buddhist's life, mediated through his or her religion. At the same time he makes it absolutely clear that Zen Buddhism and Christianity are socially and culturally distinct and different traditions. Against any uncritical plural-ist or exclusivist tendency, he also makes it clear that he is not making any judgement about the salvific efficacy of Zen Buddhism. Correctly understood, Zen Buddhism may be false and make central truth-claims that are incompatible with Christian truths, possibly leading the devout Zen Buddhist into error and a life encouraging egoism and pride. Conversely, correctly understood, Zen Buddhism may demand from its adherents a radical and selfless love of neighbour, providing the means whereby a devout Zen Buddhist is led into a salvific state of grace – a grace which originates and is recognized by the Christian, in Christ's definitive revelation of God. Or, of course, it may be a mixture of both these aspects.

If the proper context and intentions of Rahner's notion of the anonymous Christian are understood, then the pluralist objec-tions that the term stifles dialogue and is offensive are not insurmountable. Nishitani's comments make it clear that the notion of the anonymous Christian can be appreciated, though not necessarily accepted, by non-Christians without causing offence. Despite his criticisms of Rahner, Hick himself employs the same principle to explain how humanists and atheists may be involved 'without knowing it, in the transition from self-centredness to Reality-centredness; and the religious com-munities have a mission to show them the further dimensions of reality of which they are at present unaware.'[26]

The nature of religious belief

At this stage exclusivists may object that the totalitarian nature of religion is improperly obscured in Rahner's analysis. They argue that Rahner creates an existential disruption within non-Christians, by facilitating a situation where their beliefs are deemed to be ultimately untrue, while nevertheless commending the goodness of their lives. Surely beliefs and actions are intimately related and the acceptance of grace cannot be divorced from confession to the truth?[27] Is Rahner in danger of contradicting his own emphasis on the social nature of religion? Can an incorrect belief really lead to right action, eliciting selfless love and charity?

To answer these difficulties I shall consider a number of reflections offered by Rahner. First, there are situations in which actions and beliefs conflict against each other, unknown to the person. In such situations an implicit acceptance of truths may occur, *despite* objectively false professions of belief. Rahner gives the example of a materialist who denies the inner subjectivity and freedom of the human person. According to Rahner, such a materialist is in good faith capable of giving false theoretical explanations of his or her own intellectual acts; i.e. what is experienced (subjectivity and freedom, which makes possible such intellectual acts), is translated into false objective concepts and statements when the person denies their freedom and subjectivity.[28] In this example, Rahner is trying to highlight the dipolar nature of knowledge – its subjective and objective aspects. He does this to emphasize that the fundamental acceptance of God does not take place primarily in terms of accepting explicit propositional statements, but in the exercise of a life of grace.[29] At the same time, as we have seen above, Rahner still insists on a certain correlation between sincerely held correct beliefs and the exercise of a life of grace. These considerations illuminate the necessity for mission – so that an anonymous Christian may come correctly and objectively to understand the grace-filled life that is his or hers and be further shaped and guided into that life of grace. If there is a genuine tension between subjectively lived knowledge and the objectified expression of it, then such a situation should not be considered an objection to Rahner's thesis but the acknowledgement of a possible state of affairs.

Rahner's recognition of the significance of the way in which a *life is lived*, and not only of what is believed, is an important contribution to the debate. He avoids purely doctrinal contrasts, while at the same time substantiating and putting into its proper theological perspective the sometimes entirely experiential pragmatist or psychologically based criteria used by pluralists. We saw how pluralists argued that God's presence was often discernible in their meetings with non-Christians. Rahner seems to do full justice to these observations while drawing out the theological ramifications in quite a different fashion, thereby avoiding some of the difficulties the pluralists consequently encounter.

The second step in the argument against the charge of existential disruption follows on from this discussion. Kraemer's hermeneutical sensitivity to the complex difficulties in properly understanding the beliefs and motivations of other religions has been noted. Rahner makes a pertinent hermeneutical observation in the same vein, which has repercussions for dialogue as well as for the sometimes all too easy assertions of similarities or differences between religions.

Although Rahner uses the example of an atheist to make his point, this observation can clearly be extended to others. Experienced in dialogue with atheists, Rahner argues that one cannot simplistically criticize the atheist as someone who denies God for it is possible that he or she: 'merely denies something which does not exist even in the opinion of the theist who really understands his theism or who – in the dialogue with the atheist – comes to understand it properly for the first time or at least more radically than he had up to that moment'.[30] This hermeneutical sensitivity is a salutary warning to those who argue that Rahner's theory entails an existential disruption between beliefs and practice. There are complex hermeneutical problems involved in properly understanding another's beliefs, and not until this task is painstakingly achieved can legitimate examples of existential disruption be isolated. And if they are isolated, as was shown above, this does not necessarily invalidate Rahner's contentions.

The view of the Christian's self-discovery in dialogue quoted above counters the one-sided, paternalistic notion of dialogue attributed to Rahner. It highlights the dialectical structure between self-understanding and understanding of the other. In dialogue, not only can Christians learn from and about their partner, but they may also begin to learn and discover much about their own Christian faith. There are numerous testimonies to this kind of experience from those involved in interreligious dialogue.[31] It may be noted that Rahner fails to point out that such growth between and within partners in dialogue often occurs on a number of levels other than *intellectual* self-understanding. Such developments may occur in methods of prayer and meditation, architectural and artistic symbolism, and various customs and practices which can all increase self-understanding and understanding of the other.

A further point concerning dialogue arises from the complexities involved in understanding another person's religion. Besides the differences within a religious tradition, there are a number of indispensable skills (philosophical, psychological, philological, historical, sociological, to name a few, and most importantly imaginative skills) involved in 'understanding the stranger'.[32] For one person to master all these skills, especially today, is virtually impossible, 'not merely in principle but also in practice'.[33] Yet, dialogue takes place between individuals. Here Rahner is keenly aware that dialogue must begin with persons and not with systems. However, he turns this daunting task into a motivation for further dialogue – contrary to pluralist charges. The difficulties involved in properly understanding the partner's religion gives dialogue 'a meaning before any agreement is reached; viz: that one can learn an infinite amount from each other'.[34]

From all that has been said above, it would seem that the inclusivist position does justice to the different aspects involved in dialogue. Contrary to pluralist charges, it does not involve a stalemate in dialogue or imply disrespect or arrogance. Rahner is also clear that practical cooperation is not only permissible but demanded from the Christian vocation itself.[35] Contrary to exclusivist charges against the notion of the anonymous Christian, it does not completely sever the relation between beliefs and practice, acknowledging that, in some instances, this is possible while, in other cases, there may be complex difficulties involved in properly understanding the beliefs of another. Rahner is also careful to state that both beliefs and practices may be erroneous and sinful, acting as obstacles, rather than mediators of grace. Hence, inclusivists can enter dialogue in an attitude of *open commitment*. The notion of the anonymous Christian encourages a receptivity and attentiveness to the partner, knowing already that God may be present to non-Christians in their lives and religion. At the same time this very openness implicitly involves commitment, the internal logic so often obscured by pluralists. To recognize the Spirit of God at work throughout history, the Christian uses the only criteria possible: Christ and his presence within the Church mediated through the Spirit. As Kraemer so powerfully argued, any Christian criterion that does not start at Christ may be questioned as to its source and legitimacy. However, unlike Kraemer and Barthian exclusivists, Rahner uses this criterion both to question other religions (Kraemer), as well as to affirm much that is within them (Hick).

Furthermore, open commitment is also facilitated through Rahner's phenomenological sensitivity to the problems of understanding other religions. While admitting that in certain circumstances an either–or model of truth is appropriate and in others a both–and, his understanding of the Christological criterion allows for a genuine phenomenological openness. This openness is not found in Kraemer and is misguided in Hick. Although Rahner does not fully develop the implications of this open commitment, as I shall be doing in the next chapter, his realization of the need to properly encounter another religion before making any evaluations or judgements facilitates an openness to future history found lacking in Kraemer's approach. New tendencies within other religions may arise in the future and the Christian is required to enter ever anew into dialogue and confession with all.

At this point of the discussion Rahner must face a further question from pluralists. Is he genuinely open to other religions in the light of his first thesis concerning Christianity as the absolute religion and Christ as the absolute and definitive bringer of salvation? And from the opposite camp of exclusivists, Rahner must face the criticism that the very notion of anonymous faith and anonymous Christianity compromises the nature of Christian faith, which requires explicit confession and submission to Jesus. After all, the name 'Christian' designates the new relationship that a person has with God through Christ. Kraemer's view, that Christian conversion involves a radical discontinuity with one's past life, focuses upon this problem: the notion of the anonymous Christian obscures this new life, this new living in the 'mind of Christ'.[36] These very different criticisms take us back to the issue of Christology and ecclesiology.

Christology and ecclesiology

Imperialistic or reductive   It is interesting to note that these two criticisms amount to the pluralists charging Rahner as an exclusivist (only through the grace of God in Christ); and the exclusivists charging Rahner as a pluralist (obscuring the distinctiveness and *sui generis* character of Christ and Christianity)! I shall investigate the pluralist criticism first.

However open to history Rahner really seems to be, does his affirmation that God is irreversibly and definitively revealed in Christ, expressed in his Church, amount to an exclusivist-type judgement upon non-Christian religions, as his first thesis suggests? In some respects Kraemer partially addressed this question. He acknowledged the particularity of the Christian starting point. He also shrewdly noticed that pluralists also adopt specific and particularist criteria – be they a mystical experience, Jungian psychology, or Jamesian pragmatism. But if the truth of God is at stake, then Kraemer openly acknowledges that, as a Christian, he can only start from Christ and nowhere else. He also asks Christian pluralists from where their truth criteria derive.

Rahner is in complete agreement with Kraemer on this point, but goes further. He also starts from the revelation of God in Christ: 'God's promise of himself as our salvation has become in Jesus a historical event in a unique and irreversible way.'[37] Up until this event a genuine ambiguity existed. In this event the tangibility of 'God's will to save' all persons, the outcasts and the wicked, the sinners and the broken, became irreversibly present in history.[38] But Rahner goes further than Kraemer in identifying the bearers, preservers and the socially visible presence of this message with the community of the Church. In effect, Christ's presence resides, although it is not totally identified, within his Church. Without Christology there is no ecclesiology, and without ecclesiology there is no Christology.

However, to be fair to some pluralist critics, Rahner does not make it clear enough whether the normativeness of Christ precludes the possibility of future history challenging and questioning this normative status, however unlikely this may be.[39] Rahner sometimes writes as if the Christian's conviction was impenetrable to critical and historical questions, although in the wider context of his work this does not seem to be the case. I would suggest that a viable inclusivist position, while retaining the normative ontological significance of Christ, cannot claim a privileged vantage point beyond history. This is not in contradiction to the eschatological character of the Christian faith, but remains true to its historical nature. In trusting commitment Christians may affirm that, until they discover otherwise, they are convinced that God has most clearly and definitively revealed himself in the particularities of the life, death and resurrection of Jesus.

There are still two further Christological points worth noting in relation to the pluralist charge. First, Rahner's emphasis on the centrality of Christ does not impose a rigid or narrow Christocentricism as was the case with Kraemer. Although Rahner affirms the Christological teachings of Chalcedon, in his discussion of Christology he argues for the legitimacy of a plurality of Christological models within Christianity. The majority of New Testament scholars acknowledge that such a Christological plurality existed within the earliest New Testament communities.[40] Rahner goes on to argue that in the light of the varying cultural and philosophical backgrounds of Christian communities today, the affirmation of the definitiveness of Christ may legitimately take on different forms of expression. The sticking point for any Christology – and this has also been the burden of my argument in the previous chapters – lies in the affirmation that in Jesus, God is *definitively* revealed (though not necessarily exclusively revealed).[41] Hence, Rahner can say that even those who do not accept the classical formulations of Christology, perhaps because for them the classical formulations represent a square-circle dilemma, may nevertheless affirm the incarnation when they hold to the definitive nature of Christ's revelation, and this is all-important. (We may perhaps recall Hick's dilemma in explaining his own assertions that through Jesus the Christian encounters God, after his comments that for God to be present in a man is like saying that a square is a circle.) Hence, Rahner writes that

If a person really believes with regard to Jesus, his cross and his death, that there the living God has spoken to him the *final, decisive*, comprehensive and irrevocable word, and if with regard to Jesus a person realizes that he is thereby redeemed from all the imprisonment and tyranny of the existentials of a closed and guilty existence which is doomed to death, he believes something which is true and real only if Jesus is the person whom Christian faith professes him to be. Whether he knows it or not, he believes in the incarnation of God's word.[42]

It is not within the brief of this work to justify, explain and develop these Christological comments. None of the approaches under examination questions the fact that somehow God is revealed in Christ. The crucial issue bearing upon our topic concerns the relative or universal significance of this event. Against pluralists, Rahner argues that this event must bear universal and normative significance, and the discussion within this book has also attempted to show why this is necessary. How else may the Christian claim concerning an all-loving God be grounded?

The second point to be noted is that Rahner's affirmation of the definitive status of God's revelation in Christ, maintained in the Church, does not exclude, as pluralists think, the possibility of other saviours or revelations within the different religious traditions. Here Rahner cuts against extreme exclusivist tendencies, which confuse a normative revelatory event as being the sole revelatory event. Concerning 'saviour figures', be they historical or mythological, provisional or final, Rahner writes

That religious history must be asked in kindly but precise terms whether saviour figures of this kind are to be found in it, and how . . . there is no reason to exclude such discoveries from the outset, or to write them off contemptuously, as if they stood in such contrast to faith in Jesus, as the eschatological, unsurpassable saviour, that they can only be judged negatively. Saviour figures in the history of religion can certainly only be viewed as signs that – since man is always and everywhere moved by the Spirit – he gazes in anticipation towards that event in which his absolute hope becomes historically irreversible and is manifested as such.[43]

Rahner clearly avoids the negative judgement upon all religions made by many exclusivists and refutes the pluralist objection that Christ's definitiveness excludes the possibility of other saviours. Rahner's point is that all these events of mediated grace point towards their fulfilment, completion and source in the historical meridian of Christ.

But this very continuity between Christ's revelation and other revelations takes us to the heart of the exclusivist objections against Rahner. Do the revelation of God in Christ and the Christian confession and surrender to Christ point to *discontinuity* rather than continuity; to new life rather than the explicit objectification of that which is already present in the non-Christian's life; to the *sui generis* nature of the incarnation rather than to its character as the highest or best revelation? If Rahner's Christology highlights the shortcomings of pluralist Christologies, exclusivists argue that it does not go far enough.

Discontinuity and newness versus continuity and fulfilment In examining these criticisms we come to a fundamental theological disagreement between the Christologies proposed by Kraemer and some exclusivists, and those of Rahner and other inclusivists. This difference is often the reason why exclusivists emphasize discontinuity and newness against the inclusivist emphasis on continuity and fulfilment. This divide may be usefully treated in terms of the difference between *efficient* and *final* causality.

Kraemer and other exclusivists often assume or argue that Christ is the efficient cause of grace; that is to say, an unbridgeable gap existed between God and humankind, the latter being trapped in sin and guilt with constant self-made attempts to achieve salvation, and only with the event of the incarnation does God cross the divide, so to speak. Up until then, salvation was not possible – it was won through the life, death and resurrection of Jesus. Classically, this view of our relation to God and our salvation has been expressed in terms of a satisfaction theory of atonement. From this basic premise the exclusivist position is a natural implication, as is their emphasis on discontinuity.

Rahner's fundamental objection to this satisfaction theory of atonement, classically expressed by Anselm, is that it involves the 'metaphysically impossible idea of a transformation of God', whereby the cross is seen as the 'cause of human salvation in the sense that it brought about the will to save in God which otherwise would not have existed, or that it bestowed upon men a type of salvation which takes no heed of human freedom.'[44] Furthermore, such theories involve the implausible idea that 'the one making satisfaction and the one accepting it are . . . the same'.[45]

Another objection to this theory of atonement is that it obscures 'the origin and cause of the crucifixion which is the mercy and love of God', and the mercy and love of God has in reality always been the nature of God.[46] To suggest that God's will can be changed, as the satisfaction theory does, fails to safeguard the sovereignty of God, but rather implies his capriciousness.

To these major theological objections, I would add a number of others: first, did God not reveal himself in Israel's religion; second, what of those who have never encountered the Gospel, before and after New Testament times; and third, what of the New Testament passages which testify to God's universal will to save all people and the New Testament teaching that God has never left himself without witness?

One reason why Kraemer and other exclusivists hold to their párticular model of the atonement is that it seems to offer the most feasible explanation of the venerable Christian axiom that all grace and salvation comes from God in Christ. The alternative, as Rahner acknowledges, and as Kraemer feared, seems to be a subjectivist theory of atonement. In such theories, the significance of Christ is restricted to the community of Christians alone. Troeltsch, as the first among a long line of others in this century, carried out such a relativizing process, obscuring the universal significance, and claims, of Christianity.[47]

But if Rahner is correct in raising objections against a satisfaction theory of atonement, how, if at all, can he legitimately maintain that all grace, always and everywhere, comes from God in Christ? How can a single event in history affect and be the 'cause' of salvific grace, operative before and after that event? Before examining Rahner's solution, it should be pointed out that at this point there is a divide in the inclusivist camp. Some inclusivists hold that Jesus is the normative and decisive criterion by which we may judge God's

activity in history, but do not explicitly deal with the problem of
how it can be said that all grace comes from God in Christ.[48]
Like Rahner, they maintain that God is operative within non-
Christian religions and also that he is definitively revealed in
Christ. Although these inclusivists maintain a normative
Christology, thereby avoiding certain difficulties entailed by
pluralists, exclusivists may press them as to the real meaning of
the age-long Christian axiom that salvation comes alone
through God in Christ.

Rahner tackles these questions by maintaining that Jesus is
the *final*, not *efficient*, cause of God's universal salvific will.[49] By
this, he means that God's universal love is not brought about
(efficient cause) by Jesus' death, but that Jesus' death is the
final and irreversible expression of what God has always been
doing in history (final cause), which has, up until the incarnation, been obscured by the 'ambivalence of human and divine
freedom'.[50] In this sense Jesus is the goal and high-point of
creation, the most profound and telling clue to the character of
God. It is only after the life, teachings, death on a cross, and
resurrection of Jesus that the unresolved ambiguity about
God's self-communication has been resolved, calling into
question, while also gathering up and confirming, humankind's
chequered history. But Rahner argues that the life and death of
Jesus is not merely an illustration of our salvation; it is the
cause of that salvation in the sense that it is the primary
sacramental sign of God's salvific grace. Moreover, signs have a
special causality of their own, which must not be confused with
the more common notion of mechanistic causality. Rahner
introduces the notion of 'sign' and 'sacrament' to illuminate the
causal significance of this single historical event:

> If salvation history is irreversibly directed in this sense to
> salvation, and not to damnation, through a concrete event, then
> this historically tangible occurrence must be a *sign* of the
> salvation of the whole world in the sense of a '*real symbol*', and so
> possesses a type of causality where salvation is concerned. To this
> we wish to apply a well known theological concept and call it
> '*sacramental*'.[51]

Rahner's argument requires some knowledge of modern
Catholic sacramental theology. Essentially, a sign can be

understood as a cause. For instance, the sign of baptism actually is the cause of grace, although the sign itself is caused by grace. Baptism is a sacrament, expressing its significance as a mediator of grace: it both causes and is caused by grace. A sacrament is not simply a pointer, like a notice board, but is properly a 'real symbol'. As a symbol it is actually part of, and *constitutes*, the reality it discloses. It does not simply point to a reality but is part of that reality. (It is more like an encounter with the person Jane Smith, rather than a signpost to the residence of Jane Smith.) Hence, Jesus is a real symbol, because he is 'a historical and social embodiment of grace, where grace achieves its own *fullness* of being and forms an irreversible gift'.[52] In this sense, Jesus is the primary sacrament where the sign and signified are essentially one; that is, God's saving will (the reality signified) is revealed and instantiated through Jesus (the sign). In this sense, Jesus constitutes God's saving will in history in the same way as a real symbol constitutes the reality it discloses. Consequently, Jesus is the final cause, rather than the efficient cause, of the reality signified (God's saving will), which has nevertheless always been a reality.

Therefore, the reality of grace, the reality of God's will to save, the reality of Jesus, is present, whenever and wherever a person accepts God in the depths of their being. This may happen through a total surrender in selfless-love, the trusting acceptance of death, or in a non-Utopian hope for the future (i.e. in love, faith and hope), which finds its fulfilment (hence the emphasis on continuity) in Jesus and is thereby always causally related to this event as final cause. This is why Israel's religious longings are, according to the New Testament, fulfilled in Jesus the Messiah, the Christ, the awaited one. And, in principle, this is why Jesus can be seen to be the fulfilment of all goodness and grace everywhere.

As the Church maintains, preserves and preaches Christ, Rahner's argument now comes full circle. Rahner's Christology naturally leads to ecclesiology. A critic of Rahner succinctly expresses this relationship: 'This orientation is as natural as it is necessary. As every seed seeks to become the full-grown plant, as every idea presses towards expression in word or symbol, so every experience of God seeks its full identity and self-awareness in Christ, and that means in Christ's Body, the church.'[53]

Thus, by means of the above argument, Rahner is able to explain the venerable and important Christian axiom that salvation comes through God in Christ. At the same time he can also maintain that God's grace is present in other religions. However, this extra-ecclesial grace is always causally related to Christ and his Church, even when a person has never heard of Christ – hence the term 'anonymous Christian'.

Rahner also goes some way towards meeting the objection of exclusivists concerning their emphasis on *discontinuity*. In this respect he is perhaps more dialectical than Kraemer! The reason for rejecting the verdict of total discontinuity lies in Rahner's argument that the underlying assumption of total discontinuity rests upon a sharp division between nature and grace. We saw how this division in Kraemer's thought is undermined by his notion of the *sensus divinitatis* and Kraemer's admission, although not always clear, that grace is present in the lives of non-Christians. Rahner argues that the notion of *pure nature*, something totally divorced and opposed to grace, is at most a limit concept. That is, pure nature cannot be isolated in a person's life because of his or her transcendental orientation to the mystery of God. An image of a two-storey house illuminates his argument. The model that emphasizes discontinuity presupposes this two-storey house, the bottom being nature and the top, like an unrelated addition, representing supernatural grace, added on, so to speak. But because men and women are created in the image of God, as the Eastern Church so constantly reminds us, this double-decker model should be abandoned while avoiding the danger of conflating the distinction between human freedom and God's grace. Instead we should talk about graced nature rather than opposing nature to grace without precluding the possibility of a person's free rejection of grace. Consequently, if we acknowledge the possible free acceptance of grace in the non-Christian's life and therefore, by implication, mediated in part through his or her religion, then the distinction between natural religions (non-Christian religions) and the supernatural religion of Christianity must be jettisoned. The distinction between a single *sui generis* revelation in Christ and no other salvific revelation must also be jettisoned, as must the notion that all non-Christian religions are only human efforts at salvation.

The real difference between Christianity and other religions, and herein lies *discontinuity*, is located in the *Church* of Christ. The Church constitutes the 'historically and socially constituted explicit expression' of God's self-communication, which may be present in fragmented and imperfect ways outside the Church. It is a vanguard community proclaiming and striving to make present the reality that God's kingdom has come in the person of Christ.

Throughout the previous chapters I have tried to show that the issues of salvation, Christology and ecclesiology are inseparable. Much of chapter 2 was devoted to pointing out the impossibly difficult situation arising within the pluralist position in its acceptance of God's universal salvific will, normatively and ontologically, without accepting as normative and ontologically binding the events which sustain and make plausible the assertion of God's universal salvific will. Consequently, the life, death and resurrection of Jesus, communicated, preserved and present in the community founded as a result of this event, are seriously minimized in the pluralist paradigm. In effect, the pluralist position presupposes that we may know something to be true, while denying the validity and normative status of those events that reveal and are part of that truth!

For the Christian, Christology and talk of God cannot be severed, and for Rahner neither can Christology and ecclesiology. Hick's Copernican revolution sought to remove Christ and the Church from the centre and replace it with God. Kraemer's emphatic stress on the starting point of Jesus, as disclosing our knowledge of God, put Christ back into the centre. And Rahner's equally emphatic stress that we cannot talk about Christ without the Church also puts Christianity back into the centre, thereby highlighting the difficulties of a theocentric pluralism and a bare exclusivist Christocentricism. The very documents from which our knowledge of Jesus derives were written by the first Christian communities. The authenticity of these same documents (the formation of the canon) stems from the authority within the Christian community; the same authority which preserves truth within the Church – deriving from the Spirit of God.

At this point it will be useful to clarify and develop the relationship between ecclesiology and Christology in order to substantiate and illuminate the inclusivist position I am defending. As the subject of ecclesiology is a vast and complex one, I can only offer a number of considerations which affect this issue. Two particular questions demand attention. First, in the light of criticizing Kraemer's sharp distinction between Christology and ecclesiology, how can we maintain that Christ is present, as a visible sign, in his Church? Furthermore, in the light of the many appalling sins and errors of individual Christians and communities of Christians, is it plausible to maintain that the Church is the historically and socially visible sign of Christ's presence? Indeed, this latter question is certainly a stumbling block for many Christians. Before giving the outlines and principles involved in answering these questions, it should be noted that many of Rahner's ecclesiological reflections are from within a Roman Catholic context and in this respect it will be inappropriate to pursue further questions concerning the infallibility of the Pope and the sacramental and institutional indefectibility of the Church. These issues certainly demand more precise reflection, but in a book such as this, I can only indicate the general lines of an answer which may be acceptable beyond the Roman Catholic communion, although certainly the various Christian communities would need further to clarify these issues, a process which has thankfully already begun.

Newbigin argued that Kraemer's distinction between Christ's revelation and the community which exists by and for this event arises because of his neglect of the interaction between revelation and interpretation. In effect, there can be no revelation without someone expressing, remembering and transmitting it. Quite rightly, Newbigin goes on to point out that the claim for the normativeness and decisiveness of Christ 'for all human life is a meaningless claim except as it is interpreted in the life of the community which lives by the tradition of the apostolic testimony'.[54]

In as much as the Christian community lives by, interprets, remembers and practises the Gospel, it makes present in history the sign and proclamation of Christ. If the nature of the historical community which transmits and lives by this message is minimized, the Christian faith can easily turn into that which it is not: an ideal, a memory, a theory, or a code of ethical directives. Although it contains these elements, the Church is primarily a community called by God to adore his mystery, do his will and participate in his love, in humility, repentance and trust. The Church is the community 'who hear the word of God and do it' (Luke 8:21). It should be strongly emphasized that this model of the Church (and a variety of models is necessary to bring out the many aspects of the Church[55]) depends entirely on God's promise and covenant with his people and not on the strength of men and women. Therefore, properly expressing the social and historical significance of the Church, Newbigin writes that those who are Christians 'are chosen not for themselves but for the sake of doing God's will, as *witnesses* and *signs* and *agents* of his saving purposes'.[56] In this respect the Church cannot be totally divorced from Christ, but then Newbigin significantly adds that 'if they [Christians] forget this, they themselves will be rejected'.[57]

Despite the promise of the Spirit to guide and sustain the Christian community, can the Church be said to be the visible and tangible sign of God's definitive expression when it is composed of so many weak, frail and sinful people? A number of different responses are possible, such as making a distinction between the visible Church (those who belong in name) and the true invisible Church (of real Christians – a kind of anonymous Christianity within Christianity!); or the total rejection of any such claim for the Church. Rahner, however, makes the telling point that a 'Church of sinners is itself a piece of the Church's consciousness of her faith'.[58] Rahner rejects any reified or idealistic notion of the Church to safeguard his initial contention, and here he keeps company with a number of exclusivists, including Newbigin.[59] The Gospel proclamation is one of forgiveness and repentance, hence Rahner rightly says: 'Only if the Church recognises herself to be the Church of sinners will she be permanently convinced of the fact, and aware of the full force of the *obligation* it entails, that she has constant need of being cleansed, that she must always strive to do penance and achieve reform.'[60]

Clearly, the Christian community must be its own sharpest critic, always alert to the many ways in which she may obscure her own nature and 'incarnational dynamism'.[61] Not until the universal Church, in its entirety, explicitly and consciously rejects the Gospel and Christ, would its character as a sign for the world be rendered totally invalid. It will not be possible to pursue the question as to the real and precise conditions for this possibility.[62]

Consequently, real discontinuity is located in the social and historical sphere (the categorial), in the Church of Christ and not in the fact that God's saving grace is absent from all religions apart from Christianity. Hence the qualifying adjective *anonymous* (in 'anonymous Christian') expresses this crucial insight that 'in the case of a Christianity asserted to be present in this way something is missing from the fullness of its due nature, something which it should have and towards which the nature already present is tending'.[63]

At this point, exclusivists have further argued, as did Kraemer against the inclusivism of Farquhar, that the importance of mission is compromised. What is the importance of conversion if it only means coming to have the correct self-consciousness of what you already are? Furthermore, in admitting a pluralism of paths to salvation by designating non-Christian religions as 'lawful', Rahner relativizes the Church and the Gospel.[64] We have touched upon this same issue from another angle, in that this is the converse criticism of pluralists who see Rahner as a Christian triumphalist!

Mission: the redundancy of evangelization?

Before taking up these criticisms, it must be stressed, more than Rahner has done, that his reflections on the non-Christian religions concern *a priori* possibilities. Consequently, Rahner is not affirming that everyone is an anonymous Christian, but that anyone may be an anonymous Christian. He is not affirming that all religions are lawful, but that in principle this is quite possible with certain qualifications.

With this in mind, I will reiterate three reasons offered by Rahner for rejecting exclusivist criticisms concerning the redundancy of mission. Besides the fact that the duty of the Christian's own faith demands witness and proclamation, to say that conversion, for Rahner, is simply the bringing forth of the correct self-consciousness minimizes what Rahner calls 'incarnational dynamism'. This refers to the principle that the inner nature and dynamic of grace requires and seeks objectification in the social structure of a person's life. This is why the grace that is operative within the non-Christian seeks its correct objectification, through its dynamic orientation, in Christ and the Christian Church. Admittedly, Rahner does not adequately stress that this orientation is often frustrated in non-Christian religions through the effects of humankind's sinful disobedience, or the absolutizing of only aspects of truth, thereby distorting and impeding a movement towards the whole truth. This type of impediment often entails psychological, cultural and philosophical factors.[65] Furthermore, others better informed than Rahner about non-Christian religions have shown that this 'dynamic orientation' is not always historically discernible or even existentially present. Hogg's perceptive criticisms of Farquhar's fulfilment thesis regarding Hinduism is a case in point: 'Doubtless Christ fulfils what is good in Hinduism. But then he leaves out so much of what was in Hinduism, and he fulfils so much of what has never been in Hinduism, that Mr Farquhar's tracing out of the aspects of fulfilment sometimes seem far-fetched.'[66]

In this respect, Rahner may be properly accused of an undue optimism and a tendency to overemphasize fulfilment and continuity, thereby obscuring the urgency (not the necessity) of mission. When he writes that optimism is justified because God's salvific will 'is more powerful than the extremely limited stupidity and evil-mindedness of men', he is in serious danger of minimizing both the radical freedom of men and women and also the tragic effects and the extent of the 'evil-mindedness of men'.[67] In comparing Rahner with Balthasar, Rowan Williams makes some incisive remarks:

> Rahner thinks of human frustration in terms of incompletion, Balthasar in terms of *tragedy* . . . Fulfilment alone leaves the tragic problem of self-loss untouched, and so fails, in the long run, to take freedom sufficiently seriously . . . because the world is *not* a world of well-meaning agnostics but of totalitarian nightmare, of nuclear arsenals, labour camps and torture chambers.[68]

Clearly, Rahner is often guilty of overemphasizing fulfilment in a sometimes historically insensitive fashion, although, in substance, this can be rectified by focusing on a present but unduly neglected element within his inclusivist theology, that of discontinuity through sin. Furthermore, phenomenological studies do not justify an overall optimism that other religions seek their fulfilment in Christianity. Often enough they ask different questions and therefore Christ cannot be seen immediately to be their answer.

Nevertheless, and indeed because of this latter analysis, mission is seen to be a necessity not only because of the dynamic orientation of grace, but precisely because in this troubled world that dynamic orientation is so often obscured, smothered or altogether (or so it seems) absent.

The third important reason necessitating mission is expressed in a somewhat awkward manner by Rahner. He writes: 'The individual who grasps Christianity in a clearer, purer and more reflective way has, other things being equal, a still greater chance of salvation than someone who is merely an anonymous Christian'.[69] This statement has sometimes been misunderstood.[70] Rahner is clear that no guarantee of salvation is being advanced. Furthermore, he is clear that salvation is not affected by the efforts of a person but is always and everywhere the free gift of God. With these qualifications in mind, we can tease out the intention of Rahner's awkward phrase.

In the light of the explicit social and historically mediated demands of the Gospel (i.e. within the Church), the Christian can more clearly recognize the awesome demands of a God of selfless and suffering love, and be nourished and shaped in a community committed to repentance, faith, hope and charity. Because they are more explicitly shaped by and aware of the message of the Gospel, Christians may thereby use their freedom in an appropriate manner. Clearly, this does not preclude the fact that sinners exist within the Church.[71]

The converse but related side to Rahner's point is given more emphasis in his later writings, as Knitter has perceptively noted: 'More recently, [Rahner] has emphasized Christians' greater responsibility for the *welfare of others* rather than their greater *personal privilege*.'[72] Rahner has admitted that he tends to work in the tradition of 'nineteenth century individualism', too often concentrating on the *personal* rather than the *social* implications of the Church in society. A number of critics have rightly focused on this deficiency in his theology.[73]

Nevertheless, Rahner's stress on the Christian's greater responsibility for the welfare of others serves to highlight the fact that mission, service and salvation are intrinsically related in Rahner's theology, as they are for many exclusivists.

Leaving aside the problem of the most sensitive and appropriate form of mission, we may now tackle the related questions concerning the lawfulness of non-Christian religions, which exclusivists think compromise the truth of the Gospel and the Church.

First, it must be noted that Rahner stresses the possible validity of a non-Christian religion only up to the *real moment* of its existential and historical encounter with Christianity, so that 'wherever in practice Christianity reaches man in the real urgency and rigour of his actual existence, Christianity – once understood – presents itself as the only valid religion for this man, a necessary means for salvation and not merely an obligation with the necessity of a precept'.[74] This means that when a person has truly been confronted with the Gospel, without coercion or misrepresentation, and in the Gospel he or she sees the truth about themselves and God in the stark figure of the crucified Christ, then their full acceptance of the deepest demands made by this message and way of life would inevitably lead to some form of conversion. This person would then be an explicit Christian participating in the social and historical community of the Church.

The person may also possibly bring to the Church the riches and wealth of their own traditions, although clearly these elements will be transformed in their incorporation into Christianity, thereby helping to transform and properly catholicize the Church. However, it must be allowed as a possibility, which equally applies to the already confessing Christian, that a person, while fully and consciously recognizing the truth about their own nature and its orientation towards, and completion in, the mystery of God, may reject this truth. Otherwise, there would be no real human freedom. The basic meaning of sin is to be found in this act of rejection.

In the light of the above considerations, a non-Christian's continued adherence to his or her own religion would have to be considered sinful if he or she truly understood and rejected the truth of God's grace and mystery, revealed in Christ in the Christian proclamation. If this situation was existentially present (and it would be extremely difficult to locate) it would then mean that this person at that moment could not be called an anonymous Christian. However, this situation would not invalidate the lawfulness of that religion for a fellow believer who had not properly encountered Christianity. Up to the point of this real encounter, the validity or lawfulness of the religion is justified by the considerations offered above.

It is also important to note that Rahner admits that if a religion explicitly and consciously adopts as its central nature false and corrupt elements, then it could not be regarded as a lawful religion. This is reflected as the correlative of the possibility of a person's free rejection of their being, constituted by God.

The task of discerning whether a religion is lawful or not, however difficult, is left to the historian of religions. These questions, Rahner points out, can 'be answered only *a posteriori*, by the historian of religions'.[75] He also notes that this *a posteriori* investigation may well 'draw the dogmatic theologian's attention to implications in his own doctrine . . . which he had hitherto overlooked'.[76] We have already seen this in Rahner's one-sided stress on fulfilment. I will explore some further implications in the next chapter.

Finally, it should be noted that Rahner does not concede a true pluralism, in that he always affirms that all salvation is salvation through the grace of God in Christ. Pluralism only exists within this *one* plan of providential grace. It follows that Rahner has not and does not intend to relativize the Gospel and the Church. It also follows that the notion of a 'time limit' as to the validity of non-Christian religions (i.e. that they only have a limited validity up to the time of a real encounter with Christianity), often criticized by pluralists, is the necessary corollary to the first thesis concerning the definitive and normative revelation of God in Christ and his Church.

CONCLUSION

In this chapter I have tried to argue that Rahner's inclusivist paradigm provides a satisfactory reconciliation of the strengths of the pluralist and exclusivist paradigms while overcoming their shortcomings and weaknesses. This inclusivist position intelligibly reconciles and holds together the axioms of the universal salvific will of God and the axiom that salvation alone comes through God in Christ in his Church. The first axiom is used by pluralists, while severing it from its historical and normative basis. The second axiom is used by exclusivists, often at the cost of minimizing the first.

The inclusivist position also overcomes the difficulties encountered by exclusivists in explaining extra-ecclesial salvation, while also avoiding the theological confusion entailed in the pluralist recognition of this fact. Furthermore, the inclusivist stance properly affirms that the only possible normative truth criterion for Christians (as is also upheld by exclusivists) is Christ, while accommodating the suggestive insights of pluralists concerning other criteria (such as the emphasis on right action) which they sometimes fail to ground in their proper theological context. The inclusivist paradigm also offers a Christian position which is genuinely open to the history of religions without insisting on an *a priori* negative or positive judgement, although Rahner has been properly criticized for overemphasizing his optimism as to the positive outcome of this analysis.

Finally, the inclusivist position challenges the pluralist removal of Christ and his Church from the centre of the universe of faiths, and those exclusivist theologies which sever the relationship between ecclesiology and Christology.

No doubt it will have been noted that Rahner's inclusivist reflections are excessively theoretical. He cannot be blamed for this, as he offers his reflections as a dogmatic theologian, not as a historian of religions. Furthermore, there are a number of issues raised by his theory which need further exploration: what are the principles of dialogue; what is the most appropriate form of mission; what kind of truth criteria may be employed in the encounter with non-Christian religions; what of Rahner's claim that with Jesus, the end of revelation has arrived; can non-Christian scriptures and practices be legitimately used in the liturgy; in effect can Rahner's theory of the anonymous Christian gain further legitimacy from the history of religions, which in turn may raise further questions for the inclusivist position?

By way of drawing together a number of loose threads, and flushing out the implications of this kind of inclusivism, we may now, in the final chapter of this book, give shape to the implications of a viable Christian theology of religions, found, with certain qualifications, in the works of Karl Rahner.

NOTES

1. See the surveys of Race, *Pluralism*, ch. 3; Knitter, *No Other Name?*, ch. 7.
2. R. McBrien, *Catholicism* (1980), pp. 169ff.
3. Respectively, Knitter, *No Other Name?*, p. 125; Race, *Pluralism*, p. 45.
4. 'Tribute to Karl Rahner', *Heythrop Journal*, 25, 3 (1984), p. 258. For valuable introductions to Rahner's thought and life, see, H. Vorgrimler, *Karl Rahner: His Life, Thought and Works* (1965); J. Bacik, *Apologetics and the Eclipse of Mystery – Mystagogy According to Karl Rahner* (1980); H. Weger, *Karl Rahner: An Introduction to his Theology* (1980).
5. Rahner, *Spirit in the World* (1968), pp. 135–42. For a highly lucid account of Rahner's notion of *Vorgriff* see R. Williams, 'Balthasar and Rahner', in J. Riches (ed.), *The Analogy of Beauty* (1986).
6. Rahner, *Theological Investigations*, vol. 1 (1961), p. 164, n. 1.
7. Ibid., vol. 5 (1966), pp. 117–18.
8. Ibid., vol. 6, p. 391.
9. Ibid., vol. 5, p. 118.
10. Ibid., p. 119.
11. Ibid. See also Y. Congar, *The Wide World my Parish* (1961), pp. 93–115; E. Hillman, *The Wider Ecumenism: Anonymous Christianity and the Church* (1968); H. R. Schlette, *Towards a Theology of Religions*, 'Questiones Disputate' Series (1966); Küng, *On Being a Christian*, pp. 88–116.
12. Rahner, *Investigations*, vol. 5, p. 121.
13. Ibid., vol. 17 (1981), p. 42; and Knitter, *No Other Name?*, p. 117.
14. Rahner, *Investigations*, vol. 17, p. 42 (my italics).
15. Ibid., vol 5, p. 122.
16. Ibid., p. 123.
17. See G. von Rad, *The Message of the Prophets* (1968) and T. Robinson, *Prophecy and Prophets in Ancient Israel* (1953).
18. Rahner, *Investigations*, vol. 5, p. 127.
19. Ibid., vol. 5, p. 132.
20. Ibid.
21. Ibid.
22. Ibid., p. 133.
23. Hick, *God has Many Names* (US), p. 68.
24. Ibid., p. 27. For similar criticisms see Lindbeck, *The Nature of Doctrine*, p. 61; Sharpe, *Faith Meets Faith*, p. 129; Küng, *On Being a Christian*, pp. 77–8; Race, *Pluralism*, pp. 45–62.
25. Rahner, *Investigations*, vol. 16 (1979), p. 219.

26. Hick, *Second Christianity*, p. 88.
27. For instance, H. van Straelen, *The Catholic Encounter with World Religions* (1966), ch. 4; P. Hacker, *Theological Foundations of Evangelization* (1980), ch. 3.
28. Rahner, *Investigations*, vol. 9 (1972), p. 154.
29. Ibid., vol. 4 (1966), ch. 7; vol. 6, ch. 16.
30. Ibid., vol. 6, p. 38.
31. To cite only a few examples. With Hinduism: Swami Abhishik-tananda, *Hindu-Christian Meeting Point* (1969), and *An Indian Benedictine Ashram* (1964). With Buddhism: W. Johnston, *Silent Music* (1974), *The Still Point: Reflections on Zen and Christian Mysticism* (1970); T. Merton, *Zen and the Birds of Appetite* (1968). With Islam: K. Cragg, *Sandals at the Mosque* (1959), and *The Call of the Minaret* (1965). With Judaism: P. Borchsenius, *Two Ways to God: Judaism and Christianity* (1968); C. Klein, *Anti-Judaism in Christian Theology* (1978). With African religions: E. Hillman, *Polygamy Reconsidered* (1975); A. Shorter, *African Culture and the Christian Church* (1973). With atheism and secularism: H. Cox, *The Secular City* (1965); R. Garaudy (ed.), *From Ana-thema to Dialogue* (1967).
32. See N. Lash's excellent essay 'Understanding the stranger', in *Theology on Dover Beach* (1979), pp. 60–77.
33. Rahner, *Investigations*, vol. 6, p. 39.
34. Ibid., p. 40.
35. Ibid., vol. 9, p. 203.
36. Kraemer, *Christian Message*, p. 415; van Straelen, *The Catholic Encounter*, ch. 4; Hacker, *Theological Foundations of Evangeliz-ation*, ch. 3; H. de Lubac, *The Church: Paradox and Mystery* (1969), ch. 4; H. von Balthasar, *The Moment of Christian Witness* (1969); J. Moiser, 'Why did the Son of God become man?', *The Thomist*, 37 (1973), pp. 301ff.
37. Rahner, *A New Christology* (with W. Thussing, 1980), p. 9; see also *Investigations*, vol. 6, p. 393; vol. 4, p. 110.
38. Rahner, *New Christology*, p. 10.
39. John Robinson, the inclusivist, is more sensitive to this future aspect: see *Truth is Two-Eyed*, p. 129.
40. See, for example, E. Schillebeeckx, *Jesus: An Experiment in Christology* (1979); and J. G. Dunn, *Christology in the Making* (1980).
41. Rahner, *New Christology*, p. 16.
42. Rahner, *Foundations of Christian Faith* (1978), p. 227 (my italics).
43. Rahner, *Investigations*, vol. 17, p. 50.
44. Ibid., vol. 16, p. 209.
45. Ibid., p. 208.
46. Ibid.

47. For Rahner's criticisms of subjectivist theories of atonement see *Investigations*, vol. 16, p. 208.
48. For example, Robinson, *Truth is Two-Eyed*; Küng, *On Being a Christian*, pp. 123–4; Schlette, *Towards a Theology of Religions*, pp. 83–93; Hillman, *The Wider Ecumenism*, pp. 81–109; W. Buhlmann, *The Chosen Peoples* (1983), pp. 207–22.
49. See p. 69 for discussion of Kraemer's understanding of efficient causality.
50. Rahner, *Investigations*, vol. 16, p. 213.
51. Ibid., p. 214 (my italics).
52. Ibid., p. 213.
53. Knitter, *No Other Name?*, p. 129.
54. Newbigin, *Finality of Christ*, p. 77.
55. See A. Dulles, *The Resilient Church: The Necessity and Limits of Adaption* (1977), *Models of the Church: A Critical Assessment of the Church in all its Aspects* (1976); Küng, *The Church* (1968); P. Minear, *Images of the Church in the New Testament* (1960).
56. Newbigin, *Finality of Christ*, p. 115 (my italics).
57. Ibid.
58. Rahner, *Investigations*, vol. 6, p. 255.
59. Newbigin, *Finality of Christ*, ch. 5; S. Neill, *Crises of Belief* (1984), ch. 9; de Lubac, *Paradox and Mystery*; Balthasar, *Christian Witness*.
60. Rahner, *Investigations*, vol. 6, pp. 291–2 (my italics).
61. See Neill, *Crises of Belief*, pp. 226ff; Lash, *Dover Beach*, ch. 9.
62. See further, Rahner, *Investigations*, vols 6, 12, 14, 20.
63. Rahner, *Investigations*, vol. 12 (1974), p. 164.
64. See the works cited above by von Balthasar, de Lubac, van Straelen and Hacker.
65. See Congar's illuminating comments and examples in *The Wide World*, pp. 116–17, 126ff.
66. A. Hogg, 'Review of J. Farquhar's *The Crown of Hinduism*', *International Review of Missions*, 3 (1914), p. 173. See also Congar, *The Wide World*, pp. 127ff; Pannenberg, *Basic Questions*, vol. 2, ch. 4; P. Tillich, *What is Religion?* (1969), pp. 88–97; C. Braaten, *The Future of God* (1969), pp. 42–6, 58–66.
67. Rahner, *Investigations*, vol. 5, p. 123.
68. R. Williams, 'Balthasar and Rahner'.
69. Rahner, *Investigations*, vol. 5, p. 132.
70. For example, E. Hillman, 'Anonymous Christianity and the missions', *Downside Review*, 84 (1966), pp. 364–70.
71. Rahner, *Investigations*, vol. 12, p. 177.
72. Knitter, *No Other Name?*, p. 130 (my italics). See Rahner, *Investigations*, vol. 14 (1976), especially ch. 18, 19.
73. See Bacik, *Apologetics* pp. 51ff, citing Metz, Ogden, Simons and

Gerken's criticisms, but arguing that the 'communal, social, and political aspects of "human experience" can be properly developed within Rahner's theology' (p. 51). Rahner acknowledges his neglect of these themes in a preface to Bacik, *Apologetics* p. ix–x.

74. Rahner, *Investigations*, vol. 5, p. 120.
75. Ibid., vol. 17, p. 49.
76. Ibid., p. 50.

CHAPTER 5

Towards a Christian Theology of Religions

The arguments and reflections in this book have led to the suggestion that an inclusivist approach to other religions provides the most satisfactory Christian theology of religions. There are, of course, a number of differences between theologians sharing this paradigm, but it has been my contention that Karl Rahner's theory of the anonymous Christian provides a sound starting point to pursue a number of further theological, philosophical and phenomenological questions which confront Christian inclusivists.

I have called this chapter *Towards*, rather than *A* Christian Theology of Religions because I am well aware that many questions are in need of further exploration before the inclusivist paradigm can be fully accepted. Indeed, many of these questions are so complex that in this final chapter I can only indicate possible avenues along which they may be further investigated. However, I will tease out some of the exciting and challenging implications of the inclusivist position, challenges which relate to issues such as dialogue, mission, truth criteria, Christology and ecclesiology. At times I will repeat conclusions and take up suggestions mentioned earlier in the book; this will allow me to draw together many of the themes with which I have been dealing.

DIALOGUE, MISSION AND THE NEW FACE OF CHRISTIANITY IN A RELIGIOUSLY PLURAL WORLD

A major issue which has emerged in the previous four chapters concerns the aims and methods of dialogue and mission. On the one hand, some inclusivists view dialogue and mission as inseparable. On the other, certain pluralists are suspicious of this so-called indivisible relationship. Nevertheless, with reservations from some exclusivists, all three groups affirm the need for cooperation and service. From an inclusivist standpoint, I want to address a single question which has many ramifications: what are the *methods* and *aims* most appropriate to dialogue?

Dialogue on two levels

Let me begin by distinguishing two levels on which dialogue can, does and should take place. By distinguishing these two levels I do not mean to imply their incompatibility. These reflections derive from people actually involved in dialogue with non-Christians, and from my own limited experience. Furthermore, it should be added that these principles for dialogue are the result of an inclusivist Christian reflection. They may be questioned and rejected by both Christians and non-Christians. However, if dialogue is real dialogue, in the course of time, modifications and reversals in what follows may be appropriate.

Dialogue between people   There are a number of reasons for this. The primary way to approach another religion is through the members of that believing community. Throughout this book I have argued that a religion cannot be isolated from its social and historical context. Religion involves *believers* practising, worshipping, theologizing, philosophizing and so on. Religions cannot be reduced to their founding event(s) or revelation, be it a founder, a text, or both; nor can they be reduced to a set of propositional statements and theories.[1] The community which transmits, maintains and interprets revelation is a crucial factor in understanding that revelation and the religious tradition(s) which spring from it. Whatever shape or form such community may take, the practising community and its traditions must be kept in the foreground. Kraemer's attention to the totalitarian nature of religion is all-important. As we meet believers from other religions, however, it becomes all too clear that the dynamic nature and complexity within a religious tradition cannot be ignored. Here, Smith's reflections on the personal appropriation of belief in interaction with an everchanging history is also important.

It may be deduced from the above that whatever paradigm we adopt, real dialogue with other religions must begin with other people – be they learned or unlearned, sinners or saints.[2] However, this starting point does not excuse Christians from acquiring the necessary skills to acquaint themselves with their partner's religion. Historical, sociological, linguistic and theological skills, to name a few, will be useful; and most importantly, imaginative and sympathetic qualities will be required.[3] Because a religion is a historical and social complex, without this background the meaning, echoes and nuances in the partner's language and communication can easily be obscured. On a basic level, if you do not know Tamil and meet a South Indian Saivite you are not likely to get very far! Even if you speak Tamil but do not know much about the Saiva Siddhanta tradition, the dialogue may be potentially superficial.

The reverse side of the necessity of this type of preparation is allowing the partner to speak for themself. The partner should not be labelled and imprisoned in *a priori* categories and caricatures. Simply because a person is a Muslim we should not say, 'as a Muslim, you believe in X, Y, and Z'. One of the first inclusivists of this century, Fredrick Maurice, noted that a 'man will not really be intelligible to you, if, instead of listening to him, you determine to classify him'.[4] Christians may of course ask their partner, in the course of dialogue, why they do not seem to believe in X, Y and Z. Rahner reminds us that in dialogue we may come to learn that we have always misunderstood X, Y and Z; or our partner may come to realize that they have minimized X, Y and Z. Dialogue, through this kind of personal sympathetic and mutual questioning, is a means by which we can begin to properly understand the person and their religious tradition. Hence, a basic feature of dialogue is the process of listening to, learning from and understanding our partner. This process of understanding the other is an inspiration to dialogue because 'it always gives [dialogue] a meaning before any agreement is reached; viz: that one can learn an infinite amount from each other'.[5]

Another implication of this primary personal 'I–Thou' encounter is the regard for the person as person, not as an object to be manipulated. Dialogue is not the result of theological strategy or careful planning and reflection, but is itself demanded by the Gospel, as love for one's brother or sister. It is not only a duty, but the spontaneous result of the Christian's 'new mind' in Christ. Jesus speaking to Gentile and Samaritan, male and female, rich and poor alike may be recalled. The World Council of Churches *Guidelines on Dialogue with People of Living Faiths and Ideologies* (1979) makes this point clearly: 'In dialogue Christians actively respond to the command "love God and your neighbour as yourself"'.[6] Consequently, manipulation of the partner is inadmissible; i.e. either seeing the partner solely as an object for conversion (the pluralist fear), or solely as an object to increase social cooperation and well-being (the exclusivist fear). The danger of manipulation is well illustrated in a Hindu's reply to his Bhai friend's invitation to a dialogue meeting: 'You have failed to convert us by direct methods, now you will try to manipulate us by dialogue.'[7]

Although conversion and cooperation may result from dialogue and are intimately related to the injunction 'love your neighbour', entering dialogue on a personal level for these purposes *alone* does involve seeing the person as a means to an end. (Clearly for the exclusivist who believes that their partner is damned, the person's salvation and their conversion is viewed as a legitimate end and not a means. However, we have good reason for questioning this exclusivist assumption.)

Another implication of this primarily personal I–Thou encounter is that while one truly attempts to understand the other, there is a similar obligation to express one's own most fundamental hopes, anguish, beliefs and expectations. In this respect, proclamation and confession are intrinsically related to dialogue. We have had good theological and philosophical reasons to criticize some pluralist attempts to evacuate all meaning from potentially controversial or difficult Christian claims so as to facilitate friendly relations. We have also seen good reasons for the need to express these controversial Christian claims with as much sensitivity to the thought-world and background of the non-Christian, without entailing the reductivist criterion that 'the cognitive claims of Christian tradition must somehow be true also for those of other religions if these claims are genuinely to be true for Christians!'[8] Respecting the integrity of our partner, while retaining our most cherished convictions is one important way in which mutual respect and understanding are fostered. Martin Buber, a Jewish authority on dialogue, has written that dialogue is 'speech from certainty to certainty . . . from one open-hearted person to another open-hearted person. Only then will common life appear, not of an identical content of faith which is alleged to be found in all religions, but that of the situation, of anguish and expectation.'[9]

A number of those involved in dialogue, both Christians and non-Christians, have expressed the conviction that truth-claims, whether ultimately conflicting or not, form an essential part of trusting and genuine dialogue. Kraemer had clearly seen this: 'The fundamental aim [of inter-religious dialogue] involves this open exchange of witness, experience, cross-questioning and listening. The seriousness of true religion demands that one shall be one's true religious self.'[10] Samartha expresses this succinctly: 'The freedom to be committed and to be open is the prerequisite of genuine dialogue.'[11]

If Buber used the term 'speech from certainty to certainty' in expressing the *conviction* and *commitment* side to dialogue, another implication of this primarily personal I–Thou encounter is, as Samartha puts it, its *openness*. One cannot trustingly and openly learn, witness and share with a partner, without ultimately putting one's own beliefs at stake. R. Sundara Rajan, a Hindu, aptly says that if 'it is impossible to lose one's faith as a result of encounter with another faith, then I feel the dialogue has been made safe from all possible risks'.[12] Kraemer and sometimes Rahner often give the overall impression that one is primarily preaching, teaching and listening – but never being deeply and fundamentally challenged. This attitude has rightly caused concern among pluralists. Although the inclusivist Christian enters into dialogue with deep commitment, it is surely possible that through the questioning by their partner, they may actually come to abandon their own beliefs and even be converted. This possibility and risk cannot be discounted if dialogue is genuinely open and trusting.

There is a further aspect to this challenge in dialogue, which is applicable to both partners. Rahner reminds us that in dialogue the Christian may also come to understand his (or her) own Christianity 'properly for the first time or at least more radically than he had done up to that moment'.[13] In this respect Panikkar has noted that dialogue is not only *inter*-religious but also *intra*-religious.[14] That is, Christians through dialogue may discover new aspects within their own tradition which have either been obscured, forgotten or were never properly present. One may almost say that if there are anonymous Christians outside the visible Church, there is also an anonymous Christianity, so to speak, within the Church! Christians from many countries have offered testimony to the new-found depths within their own tradition and faith which had been, up to the time of their meeting with people from other religions, hidden or obscured.[15]

For instance, Kenneth Cragg, in dialogue with Muslims, avoids propositional clashes. With great hermeneutical and imaginative sympathy he explores and learns from Islam about the prophetic demand for total obedience to the divine will, the majestic and reverent acknowledgement of the sovereign transcendence of God and the devotional intensity of the Sufi mystics. All these aspects remind him of the potential deficiencies and sometimes unexplored riches within his own Christian tradition. At the same time Cragg does not minimize differences.[16] In India, Swami Abhishiktananda and his successor Bede Griffiths testify that not only is there much to learn from the Hindu philosophical tradition, but the Christian Church has also much to gain from the richness of Indian art forms, sacred liturgy, postures, meditational techniques and the sanyassin's way of life. Symbolically, their Christian ashram, rather than the Portuguese colonial churches, expresses a new face of the Indian Christian Church in mission, dialogue and confession.[17] In Japan, William Johnston, in his encounter with Zen Buddhist meditation, reflects on the theological and practical implications for a Christian who wants to practise Zen as a way of deepening his own Christian faith. He also prophetically writes of the impact of Zen upon future forms of Christianity.[18]

In dialogue, *indigenization* and *mutual self-transformation* are two sides to the same coin. This dual process does and will take place on all levels, affecting philosophy, theology, liturgy and church architecture to mention only a few aspects of Church life.

These testimonies can be multiplied from around the world.

Clearly, not only is dialogue a challenge to the partner, but also a challenge to Christians to catholicize their own tradition by embracing and transforming, through Christ, all that is good, true and holy. It is interesting to note that this indigenizing aspect of dialogue has been much criticized. However, for nearly 2000 years Christianity has itself taken shape through nothing other than the process of indigenization! Surely if Aquinas utilized Plato and Aristotle, Indian Christians may legitimately utilize Sankara and Ramanuja to express the truths of the Christian faith. If the writers of the New Testament used Jewish concepts, expectations and typology to express the significance of Jesus, then biblical translations will benefit in employing non-Judaeo-Christian terminology when addressed to Buddhist or Hindu audiences. Christians translating the Bible for Burmese Buddhists have in fact employed the term *dhamma*, which is strongly akin to the Greek notion of *logos*, so that the opening of John's gospel reads: 'In the beginning was the *Dhamma*'.[19] This process of indigenization within Christian history is not confined to theology and philosophy. Cardinal Newman bears learned testimony to Christianity's history of critical synthesis, rather than uncritical syncretism. For instance, he noted that

> The use of temples, and these dedicated to particular saints, and ornamented on occasions with branches of trees; incense, lamps and candles; votive offerings on recovery from illness; holy water; holydays and seasons, use of calendars, processions, blessings on the fields; sacerdotal vestments, the tonsure, the ring in marriage, turning to the East, images at a later date, perhaps the ecclesiastical chant, and the Kyrie Eleison, are all of pagan origin, and sanctified by their adoption into the Church.[20]

Hence, through dialogue, the Christian may not only be challenged to total conversion away from Christianity, but also to a continual conversion and deepening of his or her own Christian faith.

The above insights have important repercussions for the concept of fulfilment. We have already noted that sometimes certain religions are questioned, challenged and also called to abandon their most central convictions in the light of Christ (hence fulfilment alone is not an adequate category and the notion of discontinuity may be usefully employed). Now another important qualification must be made to the idea of fulfilment. After a comprehensive and illuminating study of the way in which Christianity renews itself and grows in richness and depth through dialogue, Arnulf Camps rightly concludes: 'Thus the Church, or the Churches, is no complete fulfillment, neither is present day Christianity.'[21] Lesslie Newbigin adds this pertinent testimony:

> 'Christianity' as a historical movement is and must be a growing and developing thing. It grows and develops not merely by extending the circle of its membership, but because in the encounter of the Gospel with new cultures, new aspects of the fullness of God in Christ are brought to light.[22]

In effect, Christianity itself becomes fulfilled in and through dialogue and the process of indigenization which accompanies dialogue. No longer is it possible to say that the other religions will find their fulfilment in Christianity, without at the same time acknowledging that Christianity will also find its *own* fulfilment through a real meeting with the riches and insights within other religions.

Another qualification to the notion of fulfilment becomes evident when observing the historical process of indigenization. Newman's study makes it clear that for centuries Christianity has critically incorporated and utilized the practices, rites, prayer forms and belief systems of its non-Christian neighbours. But he also notes how all these things have been 'sanctified by their adoption into the Church'. Against Newman we must say that many rites, practices and beliefs were not without sanctity before their adoption into the Church. With Newman, however, it must be noted how the original integrity and context of these practices, rites and beliefs are fractured and dislocated as they are now seen through a new focal point – Christ. Consequently they are now related within a new complex cluster of beliefs, practices and rites which constitute the developing Christian tradition. In this sense fulfilment will often mean destruction and purgation. This aspect must be kept in mind if the notion of the anonymous Christian is to have any credence. The transition from anonymous to explicit Christianity not only involves coming to a correct self-understanding, but may also involve radically questioning and reconstructing one's previous self-understanding. *Fulfilment without discontinuity* may fail to do justice to the complexity of the situation.

To summarize: there are a number of important points that arise from an examination of dialogue on the personal level, only some of which I have outlined above. We saw that dialogue requires intellectual, imaginative and sympathetic qualities and one of its basic aims is understanding the partner and his or her religion. The inspiration for dialogue is found in the New Testament command to love God and one's neighbour as oneself, and this means that any form of manipulation in dialogue is inadmissible. But there is more to dialogue than understanding, it also involves a genuine sharing with the other of one's most cherished hopes, fears and beliefs. Without this confessional aspect, dialogue loses the sense of encounter with real people and their aspirations and tragedies.

Conflicts and disagreement cannot always be avoided. Commitment must be equally matched with openness, knowing that God may be present in the partner's life and religion. Genuine openness may lead to conversion, but it can equally lead to a multi-faceted enrichment of Christianity. Liturgy, theology, architecture and social practice can all be transformed through the encounter with other religions and only in this process can the Church find its fulfilment and catholicity.

Finally, we also noted how the notion of fulfilment must be kept in tension with the notion of discontinuity to do justice to the complexity of Christianity's relation to other religions.

Institutional dialogue Much of the foregoing applies to this second level of dialogue, in as much as persons belong to and actually form institutions and organizations. However, as institutions and groups have different sociological and psychological functions from individuals, it will be useful to offer some further reflections.

By institutional dialogue I mean dialogue between *official representatives* of different religious communities. Due to the social and communal nature of religion this institutional aspect is an important and necessary one, although the authority and jurisdiction of official representatives will vary within the different Christian denominations, as they will within the various non-Christian religious communities. There are a number of Christian bodies involved in this form of dialogue; perhaps the two most important (in terms of their numerical representation – and paper output!) are the World Council of Churches and the Roman Catholic Church.[23] Both bodies are involved in inter- and intra-religious dialogue and officially expound versions of inclusivist theology, although of course there is a plurality of opinions within these two bodies.

There are three areas of institutional dialogue upon which I will focus: the importance of *theological and pastoral guidelines* for dialogue; the *participation* of the churches in actual dialogue; and the responsibilities of the churches to *foster an environment* in which the latter objective can be maintained and encouraged.

First, large Christian communities involved in dialogue may find it useful to draw up commonly agreed theological and pastoral guidelines. These guidelines will, of course, require interpretation and application in the different contexts in which Christian communities find themselves. Christians involved in dialogue in India, Japan, China, the United States and England will find different things appropriate to their situations. Drawing up such guidelines is part of the pastoral responsibility of mature leadership concerned with unity within the Christian community. In this respect both the Roman Catholic Church and the World Council of Churches have thought through and developed the implications of an inclusivist theology in relation to dialogue. For instance, concerning guidelines for practical cooperation, the World Council raises an important point:

> Common activities and experiences are the most fruitful setting for dialogue on issues of faith, ideology and action. It is in the search for a just community of humankind that Christians and their neighbours will be able to help each other break out of cultural, educational, political and social isolation in order to realize a more participatory society. It may well be that in particular settings such common enterprises will generate interreligious committees or organizations to facilitate this kind of dialogue-in-action.[24]

Just such an inter-religious grouping came together in Colombo in 1974, where Buddhist, Christian, Hindu, Jewish and Muslim representatives produced a joint report entitled *Towards*

World Community: Resources and Responsibilities for Living Together. There have been many meetings of this kind.

There are two points to be made about the World Council of Churches' statement quoted above. First, it indicates that Christians must participate in the creation of a just society. Rahner reminds us that there can be no Christian blue-print for the concrete future organization of society. In this respect, he writes that if 'Christianity as such demands no *particular concrete* future . . . Why not try together to come to a clearer awareness of those hoped-for aspects of the future which have as yet been anticipated only dimly – justice, freedom, dignity, unity and diversity in society?'[25] Although there are good theological reasons for Christian involvement in society (and both the World Council and Roman Catholic Church are clear about this), there is also a host of complex and difficult issues that lies ahead.

This brings us to my second point. Cooperation can sometimes lead to the highlighting of differences. On the practical level these differences may be irresolvable and, on the theological level, they may raise disturbing and challenging issues concerning truth-claims. For instance, if two religious communities constitute the main population of a country there may be sharp differences about the meaning of 'justice'. Although there are a variety of interpretations and practices among Muslims concerning the *Haad* offences – stoning for adultery, 80 lashes for the false accusation of adultery and drinking wine, amputation of either hand or foot, or both, for theft or highway robbery – Christians, for instance, may find themselves opposed to an important aspect of Muslim belief and practice when cooperating in formulating or implementing legislation in that country. Examples of possible conflicts can be multiplied, concerning issues at every level of society, such as education, law, health and morality.[26] Similarly, certain Christian beliefs and practices may equally cause offence to non-Christians. The Holy Spirit may well be working through the non-Christian partner to judge and to convict the Church, so any offence must be considered seriously. At other times, genuinely irresolvable differences and conflicts may emerge which possibly reflect ultimately opposing perceptions of truth.

In the same way that cooperation can bring about better understanding, harmony and tolerance, it can also highlight differences, disagreements and sometimes permissible levels of 'intolerance'. Perhaps the outlawing of the already-then-waning Hindu practice of *sati* (widow burning) in British-ruled India is a case in point. These issues are complex and difficult and mutual cooperation, however positive sounding, is fraught with ambiguities, peril and promise. What I wish to reiterate, and both the World Council and Roman Catholic guidelines emphasize this, is that cooperation and service are demanded by the Christian Gospel and are intrinsically related to witness, mission and dialogue.

Having considered the importance of theological and pastoral guidelines, I will now consider another aspect of institutional dialogue: the actual *participation* of the churches in dialogue. It is one thing for the churches to draw up guidelines and another for them to become involved and participate in dialogue.

In the 1960s the Indian Roman Catholic hierarchy in India set an encouraging example. If dialogue is to be thorough and genuine, then it requires entire church communities and not only isolated individuals to participate and think through the issues. Fr D. S. Amalorpavadass, for example, headed the official Roman Catholic National Biblical, Cathetical and Liturgical Centre in Bangalore, developing a theology of mission and indigenization which was as far reaching in its effects as it was radical. The Centre produced *New Orders for the Mass in India*. Here the daily office included passages from the Old Testament, New Testament, the Church fathers *and* the Hindu sacred texts.[27] An Indian *anaphora* was also implemented.

These and many other important theological and pastoral innovations, which had the support of the hierarchy, are justified by Amalorpavadass in his vision of the future of the Christian Church (in India), as passing 'from a notion of the Church that is sectarian and parochial, territorial and static, introverted and imported, to a notion that is catholic and universal, authentic and interior, adult and dynamic.'[28]

In the 1970s, however, South Indian Christians, deeply attached to the Latin liturgy, opposed the use of non-biblical scriptures and an Indian *anaphora*. Again we witness the promises and peril of dialogue. Although in 1975 Rome forbade the use of non-biblical scriptures and an Indian *anaphora* in deference to the scandalizing of the faithful, the new order is widely practised and sanctioned in experimental centres and for private use.[29]

Whether Rome was right in doing this, clearly there are particular institutional responsibilities and difficulties facing Church leaders. On the one hand, they must guard against scandal and uncritical syncretism. On the other, they must encourage and implement the legitimate aspirations for an indigenous Church and real dialogue. Both these aspirations were sanctioned by Vatican II. Reflections on the theology of religions will be valuable in guiding the organizational body of the Christian Church in situations of dialogue, and in response to the pastoral needs of various communities.

If the first point concerned the provision of guidelines for dialogue and the second concerned the institutional involvement in dialogue, the third and final point concerns the responsibilities of the churches to foster an environment in which the long-term process of inter-religious dialogue may be maintained and encouraged. This goal can be achieved through a number of channels, education being a primary one. The World Council guidelines express this clearly:

> Dialogue should generate educational efforts in the community. In many cases Christians, utilizing the experience of dialogue, must take the initiative in education in order to restore the distorted image of the neighbours that may already exist in their communities and to advance Christian understanding of people of living faiths and ideologies.[30]

The document goes on to list how this should be done, from primary to adult levels of education, in both 'secular' and 'religious' institutions.

This process will inevitably raise certain difficulties. The passage above, from the World Council guidelines, goes on to state that it will be necessary to review 'material used and teachings customarily given in courses of instruction at all levels'. Although the Council applies this stricture to religiously maintained bodies, it may be argued that it should equally be applied to all educational establishments. But even within Church colleges, questions may arise as to whether an uncompromising and harsh form of exclusivist theology runs contrary to this goal; or whether, for instance, the religion of the

Unification Church should be treated equally with modern day Japanese Buddhism; or should education be presented in a neutral phenomenological fashion or whether this is even possible or ultimately desirable.[31] The problems are legion. Nevertheless, they must be faced if the churches are truly committed to fostering an environment in which dialogue may be maintained and encouraged.

Another problem here related to the fostering of an environment in which dialogue is facilitated, concerns the pressing practical issue of whether joint worship and prayer is possible, or even desirable. Again, the inclusivist guidelines of the World Council perceptively note that working together 'will eventually raise the very difficult and important question of fuller sharing in common prayer, worship or meditation'. The guidelines also acknowledge that this 'is one of the areas of dialogue which is most controversial and most in need of further exploration'.[32] It is interesting to note that the Roman Catholic Church, usually so cautious and careful, in its guidelines on relations with Jews, states that

> In whatever circumstances as shall prove possible and mutually acceptable, one might encourage a common meeting in the presence of God, in prayer and silent meditation – a highly efficacious way of finding that humility, that openness of heart and mind, necessary prerequisites for a deep knowledge of oneself and of others.[33]

The Catholic Church goes further in clarifying this issue in a document concerning Christian–Muslim dialogue. It makes it clear that involvement in the official cultic worship of the Muslim religion would be both dishonest and inappropriate, for this would involve the Christian in identifying with the totality of that religious tradition. But it also recognizes an important area that can be further explored:

> Apart from special and very rare occasions, when certain prayers drawn from one or other religious heritage could be said in common, it would seem preferable to compose special prayers, which can express the religious sentiments of all those taking part, whether Christian or Muslim; prayers based on common beliefs.[34]

How this directive could be applied to fundamentally non-theistic religions remains an open and challenging question. Concerning joint prayer and worship, it would be rash to say anything more than that Christians involved in such intimate dialogue may be best placed to judge upon the prudence of such joint worship – while always keeping the wider theological issues in mind. It would also be rash to say anything less than that this issue cries out for further attention.

Conclusion

In this examination of the complex issues of dialogue, mission and ecclesiology from an inclusivist standpoint, there are a number of points worth summarizing. It is impossible to separate dialogue, mission and service. If dialogue is reduced to social service, then the important area of religious truth-claims is ignored and with it, the heart of a person's religious life and commitment. We also have reason to believe that mutual cooperation will often lead to wider questions concerning matters of truth, such as: 'What is the purpose and nature of men and women?'; 'What is their relationship to their environment and to each other?' If dialogue is reduced to preaching alone, however, then the concrete and practical aspects of Christian witness, which include social service, are ignored with the consequence of a dangerous 'spiritualizing' of salvation; i.e. salvation is given purely other-worldly meaning, rather than its proper biblical concern with every aspect of being human. Furthermore, if dialogue is truly dialogue, Christians and their Church communities will undergo a sometimes painful, but also creative and transformative, metamorphosis. Dialogue is not only inter-religious but also intra-religious. For this reason (among others) the Church cannot be fully characterized as the final fulfilment of non-Christian religions, for it will, itself, undergo fulfilment through dialogue. Dialogue will no doubt always provide promise and peril in equal measure.

JESUS AND CHRISTIAN TRUTH CRITERIA

It is appropriate to conclude this final chapter with some

comments on Christian truth criteria in the face of dialogue
with non-Christian religions. I have argued throughout this
book that there are good grounds to maintain that ultimately
Christ is and must be the *definitive* truth criterion for Christians. However, it is difficult to claim, as some exclusivists do,
that this valid criterion disqualifies all other events in history
from being regarded as part of God's saving plan. It is also
difficult to claim, as some pluralists do, that one can recognize
God's action everywhere in history without a normative
revelatory event in which God is definitively revealed and
recognized. Furthermore, the normative revelation of God in
Christ should not be viewed entirely as a matter of affirming
propositional truth-claims, but also involves the recognition
that the *practice* of true charity, faith and hope implicitly
requires the grace of God in Christ. In this respect, truth is also a
matter of doing, not only of knowing.

All these contentions, for which I have argued in the course of
this book, have a number of implications in terms of an
inclusivist affirmation that Jesus is the definitive truth criterion. I shall only indicate some of these implications.

Discovering, while utilizing the Christological criterion

First, there will sometimes be situations when an either–or
model of truth is necessary to explain conflicting truth-claims.
There will also be situations when a both–and model will be
necessary to explain what turn out to be only *apparently*
conflicting truth-claims. Even in this latter case, the normativeness of Christ is significant in as much as complementary
truths can only and ultimately be an aspect of one and the same
truth of God in Christ. One cannot harmonize truth-claims if
they fundamentally contradict the revelation of God in Christ.
It must also be remembered that complementary insights, if
they are to be genuinely valid, cannot be detached from the
whole in which they have their meaning. In this respect, certain
continuities may often best be viewed in the light of disconti-
nuities as well, and certain complementary aspects in the light
of wider contradictions.

As Trinitarian and ecclesiological reflections are properly
focused and grounded in Christ, the normativeness of Christ
must always be the implicit or explicit criterion when reflecting

upon and evaluating the insights from other religions concerning the nature of God, the human person and the world. These terms may be inappropriate for certain religions, although it is the reality signified by them that is at stake. Such a task, with all its nuances and complexities, is undertaken by Camps when he tries to 'get to the core of other people's views of God, humanity and the world'.[35] As a Christian, he examines Islam, Hinduism, Buddhism, the new Japanese religions, folk religions in Latin America and Maoism, 'starting out with the salvific data and values [Christians] possess in Christ'.[36] By utilizing the Christological truth criterion in this way, Camps is able to trace elements of continuity and discontinuity, truth and error, within other religions. And, as was seen earlier in this chapter, the use of this criterion also entails a situation in which the depth and richness of the Christological criterion itself becomes evident. This is exemplified in Camps' investigations.

We saw, on the one hand, how Kraemer's excessive emphasis on a Pauline Christology blinded him to certain aspects of light and goodness within other religions. On the other hand, we also saw how Rahner pointed out that there may be a legitimate plurality within Christology as long as the centre and starting point of these reflections recognizes Jesus as the definitive revelation of God. Hence, a complex and somewhat paradoxical process of *discovering, while utilizing* the Christological criterion takes place in dialogue.

The values, truths and insights possessed in Christ not only question, but are also enlarged and enriched through meeting people from other religions. The new depth of this Christological criterion is found, not only in terms of sometimes neglected issues such as the value of the impersonal, the place of evil and the importance of the feminine (as Robinson has shown in his encounter with Hinduism), but also in terms of the various indigenous forms of expressing Christ's significance and meaning, as Camps and others have discovered.[37]

Truth and practice

There is a further point to be noted regarding this truth criterion. Because of the priority of the Christological truth criterion, we are able to put into their proper theological context the pragmatic and psychological criteria employed by pluralists. These pluralist criteria are rightly criticized by Kraemer for being granted (implicitly at least) normative status. Knitter, for instance, argues that a religion is true if it promotes 'the welfare, the liberation of all peoples, integrating individual persons and nations into a larger community'.[38] Although the orientation of such a statement is correct, its theological context gives it decisive shape. It is through Christ and his community that a Christian comes to know and seek after the 'liberation' and 'welfare' of all people.

We have already noted how conceptions of justice can differ between religions. The danger of not recognizing the theological and Christological underpinnings of pragmatic truth criteria serves only to confuse or evacuate any substantial meaning from such criteria. Consequently, in the light of Christian insights into justice, freedom and liberation – and these will of course be open to correction and developments – the Christian can truly acknowledge that often and with great ardour the non-Christian is seen to be engaged in the practice of truth.

This recognition in itself raises further and more profound questions. In chapter 4 particularly we noted how difficult it is to penetrate into the subjectivity of an individual's free decision, expressed in action. However, what can be theologically stated is that all grace is the grace of God, and that grace is causally related to, and definitively expressed in, Christ. This means that the practice of charity, hope and faith by individuals within their community can also be legitimately regarded as an expression of truth, because their actions are a consequence of grace offered and implicitly accepted. Whenever a person truly gives of themselves in selfless love for another, or in acts of true faith, hope and charity, they do this by God's grace. However, and here we reach our question, if as we have seen, there may be legitimate instances where grace is mediated through and not despite the non-Christian's religion, we may ask whether and how a non-Christian rite can properly be regarded, if at all, as a sacramental mediator of grace. Certain theologians influenced by Rahner have developed some interesting lines of reflection on this question.[39] I cannot pursue this important topic here, but simply want to indicate that the practice of truth is as important and perhaps finally indivisible from the proper understanding of, and worship of, truth. If theory illuminates practice, then practice will also illuminate theory.

Jesus, the 'end' of revelation?

Another issue which is clarified when the Christological truth criterion is maintained is a proper understanding of the notion that some theologians express in calling Jesus the *end* of revelation. In the light of my extensive discussion of extra-ecclesial revelation and salvation, it is clear that the notion of the 'end' of revelation in Christ should not be literally interpreted. It should not be seen as implying that God's dealings with humankind have come to an end. In fact, within the Christian community it was held from the earliest days that a deepening and on-going understanding of truth was necessary. John's account of Jesus' words at his passion are instructive:

> I have yet many things to say to you, but you cannot bear them now. When the Spirit of truth comes, he will guide you into all the truth; for he will not speak on his own authority, but whatever he hears he will speak, and he will declare to you the things that are to come. He will glorify me, for he will take what is mine and declare it to you (John 16:13–14).

The Spirit is not the exclusive property of the Christian Church, but it is intimately related and ultimately indivisible with Christ and the Father. The Trinitarian tradition within the Church is testimony to this. In the sense that Jesus is the definitive revelation of God in history – the decisive norm by which all subsequent and previous revelations are judged and related – in this sense only can Christ be said to be the end of revelation. Although the Christian may believe that Jesus is the 'end' of revelation, this belief does not preclude the universal workings of the Spirit, which 'blows where it will'. The Trinitarian theology of Christianity helps to explain why the presence of God's Spirit in other religions is the presence of Christ. It is only through the guidance of the Holy Spirit that the Christian may discover the presence of Christ ('He will glorify me') both within and outside of the Church ('and declare it to you'). Using a phrase employed by Robinson: 'To believe that God is best defined by Christ is not to believe that God is confined to Christ.'[40]

A final and related aspect of maintaining this Christological truth criterion is its repercussions for ecclesiology. While we have had good reason to criticize the severing of Christ from the community which interprets, proclaims, and bears witness to him, we should keep in mind that the Holy Spirit through the Father and the Son is also leading the pilgrim Church into a deeper and constantly fresh understanding of its role and purpose – as it is presently doing through the encounter with non-Christian religions. The Church must also undergo constant questioning and correction and should not be falsely elevated into an invulnerable fortress of truth or into an unqualified identity with the kingdom of God. Newbigin puts it well: 'The Holy Spirit, who convicts the world of sin, of righteousness, and of judgement, may use the non-Christian partner to convict the Church'.[41] Christian communities are constantly called to be bearers of the Gospel in their lives, words and thoughts, as individuals and as communities. The inclusivist position, in its affirmation that Jesus is the definitive truth-norm, disavows any complacency or smugness, for this norm constantly demands vigilance and perseverance, while giving strength and confidence to the Christian community of saints and sinners.

CONCLUSION

Much of this chapter has indicated the truly exciting and open-ended theological and phenomenological tasks facing the Christian confronted by religious pluralism. The form of inclusivism I have argued for tries to do full justice to those two most important Christian axioms: that salvation comes through God in Christ alone, and that God's salvific will is truly universal. By maintaining these two axioms in fruitful tension, the inclusivist paradigm can be characterized by an openness and commitment; an openness that seeks to explore the many and various ways in which God has spoken to all his children in the non-Christian religions and an openness that will lead to the positive fruits of this exploration transforming, enriching and fulfilling Christianity, so much so that its future shape may be very different from the Church we know today. Such exploration will also lead to a self-discovery which can only enhance and clarify the most basic commitment of Christians,

that in Jesus Christ, God has disclosed himself as a God of
suffering and redemptive love, a suffering and redemptive love
that demands constant exploration and discovery. T. S. Eliot's
words give some shape to this exciting encounter with the non-
Christian religions:

> We shall not cease from exploration
> And the end of all our exploring
> Will be to arrive where we started
> And know the place for the first time.[42]

NOTES

1. See Lindbeck, *The Nature of Doctrine*, in which he offers an
   excellent analysis of this issue in support of the position I am
   advancing concerning the nature of religion.
2. Even conservative evangelicals now acknowledge this starting
   point, rejecting Barth's *a priorism*. See J. Stott, 'The biblical basis
   of evangelism', in G. Anderson and T. Stransky (eds), *Mission
   Trends No. 2: Evangelization* (1975): 'Dialogue becomes a token of
   Christian humility and love because it indicates our resolve to rid
   our minds of the prejudices and caricatures that we may entertain
   about the other man' (pp. 14–15).
3. See Knitter, *No Other Name?*, pp. 205–16; R. Panikkar, *Myth,
   Faith and Hermeneutics* (1979).
4. F. D. Maurice, *The Religions of the World and their Relations to
   Christianity* (1886), p. 96.
5. Rahner, *Investigations*, vol. 6, p. 40.
6. World Council of Churches (WCC), *Guidelines on Dialogue With
   People of Living Faiths and Ideologies* (1979), para 18.
7. S. Samartha, *Courage for Dialogue* (1981), p. 9.
8. Knitter, *No Other Name?*, p. 228; see also Smith, *Towards a World
   Theology*, pp. 101, 126.
9. M. Buber, *Between Man and Man* (1947), p. 24.
10. H. Kraemer, *World Cultures and World Religions* (1960), p. 356.
    See also Newbigin, *The Open Secret*, ch. 10; British Council of
    Churches (BCC), *Relations with People from Other Faiths: Guide-
    lines for Dialogue in Britain* (1983), pp. 7, 12.
11. Samartha, *Courage for Dialogue*, p. 43.
12. Cited in L. Newbigin, *Christian Witness in a Plural Society* (1977),
    p. 23.
13. Rahner, *Investigations*, vol. 6, p. 38.

14. R. Panikkar, *The Intrareligious Dialogue* (1978).
15. See chapter 4, n. 31.
16. K. Cragg, *Muhammed and the Christian: A Question of Response* (1984).
17. See my 'A Hindu Christianity', *The Tablet*, 237 (1983), pp. 1203–04.
18. W. Johnston, *Christian Zen* (1971), *The Still Point*.
19. T. Ling, *A History of Religion East and West* (1968), p. 87.
20. Newman, *The Development of Christian Doctrine*, p. 373.
21. Camps, *Partners in Dialogue*, p. 155.
22. Newbigin, *Christian Witness*, p. 18.
23. See the WCC *Guidelines on Dialogue* and the following documents of Vatican II: on 'Non-Christian Religions' (*Nostra Aetate*); 'Missionary Activity' (*Ad Gentes*); 'Church in the Modern World' (*Gaudium et Spes*) and 'Evangelism in the Modern World' (*Evangelii Nuntandi*), in A. Flannery (ed.), *The Conciliar and Post-Conciliar Documents* (1975). See also the lengthy document prepared by the Secretariat for Non-Christians (SNC), *Religions: Fundamental Themes for a Dialogistic Understanding* (1970).
24. WCC *Guidelines on Dialogue*, pt. III, no. 7. See also '*Ad Gentes*', ch. 6, no. 35–41.
25. Rahner, *Investigations*, vol. 9, p. 203.
26. See C. Lamb, *Belief in a Mixed Society* (1985) and M. Langley, *Ethical Dialogue with Other Religions* (1979).
27. D. Amalorpavadass, *Towards Indigenization in the Liturgy* (1971), and (ed.), *Research Seminar on Non-Biblical Scriptures* (1975).
28. D. Amalorpavadass, *Gospel and Culture* (1978), p. 55.
29. See Camps, *Partners in Dialogue*, pp. 193–9 and 'New dialogue with Hinduism in India', *Concilium*, 161 (1983), pp. 61–7; in the same issue, see the parallel report by J. van Bragt, 'New dialogue with Buddhism in Japan' pp. 68–73.
30. WCC, *Guidelines on Dialogue*, section III, no. 5.
31. See E. Hulmes, *Commitment and Neutrality in Religious Education* (1979); N. Smart and D. Horder (eds), *New Movements in Religious Education* (1975).
32. WCC, *Guidelines on Dialogue*, section III, no. 10.
33. 'Guidelines for Relations with the Jews', ch. II, no. 4, in Flannery (ed.), *Conciliar Documents*, p. 745.
34. SNC, *Guidelines for a Dialogue between Christians and Muslims* (1969), p. 157. n. 1.
35. Camps, *Partners in Dialogue*, p. 151. See ch. 6–13.
36. Ibid., p. 151.
37. Camps, *Partners in Dialogue*, ch. 18; S. Samartha, *The Hindu Response to the Unbound Christ* (1974); R. Boyd, *India and the*

Latin Captivity of the Church: The Cultural Context of the Gospel (1974).

38. Knitter, *No Other Name?*, p. 231.
39. See N. Abeyasingha, *A Theological Evaluation of Non-Christian Rites* (1979). I have pursued a number of these questions in 'Karl Rahner's anonymous Christian – A reappraisal', *Modern Theology*, 1 (1985), pp. 139–45.
40. Robinson, *Truth is Two-Eyed*, p. 129.
41. Newbigin, *Christian Witness*, p. 22.
42. T. S. Eliot, 'Little Gidding', in *Collected Poems* (1963).

Bibliography

All works referred to in the text are listed below under one of two classifications. The first list, Christian Attitudes to Other Religions, can serve as a bibliographical guide. This list is by no means exhaustive and I would refer the reader to my forthcoming book *Christianity and the Encounter with Other Religions: a Bibliographical Guide* (1987) for a more detailed and sectionalized bibliography.

The second list, Additional Works, will allow the reader to pursue other works cited in the text but excluded from the main bibliography.

Citations from journals have full bibliographical information given in the notes and are not referred to here, except in the case of articles by John Hick, which are included to give a more complete guide to his work.

ABBREVIATIONS

To help make the bibliography more manageable for the reader, the following abbreviations have been used:
BCC: British Council of Churches
CISRS: Christian Institute for the Study of Religion and Society
CLS: Christian Literature Society
NBCC: National Biblical and Cathetical Centre
SCM: Student Christian Movement
SNC: Vatican Secretariat for Non-Christians
SPCK: Society for the Propagation of Christian Knowledge
WCC: World Council of Churches

CHRISTIAN ATTITUDES TO OTHER RELIGIONS

Abeyasingha N., *A Theological Evaluation of Non-Christian Rites*, Bangalore, Theological Publications of India, 1979.

Abhishiktananda, Swami (H. le Saux), *Hindu–Christian Meeting Point*, Bangalore, CISRS, 1969.

Abhishiktananda, Swami and Monchanin J., *An Indian Benedictine Ashram*, Tiruchirapalli, Saccidananda Ashram, 1951; revised edn, *A Benedictine Ashram*, Douglas, Times Press, 1964.

Amalorpavadass D. S., *Gospel and Culture*, Bangalore, NBCC, 1978.
Research Seminar on Non-Biblical Scriptures, Bangalore, NBCC, 1975.
Towards Indigenization in the Liturgy, Bangalore, NBCC, 1971.

Anderson G. and Stransky F. (eds), *Christ's Lordship and Religious Pluralism*, Maryknoll, NY, Orbis, 1981.
Mission Trends No. 2: Evangelization, Grand Rapids, Michigan, Eerdmans Publishing, 1975.

Anderson J. N., *Christianity and Comparative Religion*, London, Inter-Varsity Press, 1971.
The Mystery of the Incarnation, London, Hodder & Stoughton, 1978.
(ed.), *The World Religions*, London, Inter-Varsity Press, 1975.

Appasamy A. J., *The Gospel and India's Heritage*, London and Madras, SPCK, 1942.

Askari H., see Hick J.

Barth K., *Church Dogmatics*, Edinburgh, T. & T. Clark, vol. 1/2, 1956, and vol. 4/3, 1962.

BCC, *Relations with People of Other Faiths: Guidelines for Dialogue in Britain*, London, BCC, 1983.

Borchsenius P., *Two Ways to God: Judaism and Christianity*, London, Valentine, Mitchell, 1968.

Boyd R., *India and the Latin Captivity of the Church: The Cultural Context of the Gospel*, Cambridge, Cambridge University Press, 1974.

Braaten C., *The Flaming Center: A Theology of the Christian Mission*, Philadelphia, Fortress Press, 1977.

Braybrooke M., *Inter-Faith Organizations, 1893–1979: A Historical Directory*, New York, Edwin Meller Press, 1980.
Together to the Truth: Developments in Hindu and Christian Thought since 1800, Delhi, SPCK, 1971.

Buhlmann W., *All Have the Same God*, Slough, St Paul's Publications, 1979.
The Chosen Peoples, Maryknoll, NY, Orbis, 1983.

Camps, A., *Partners in Dialogue: Christianity and Other World Religions*, Maryknoll, NY, Orbis, 1983.

Christian W., *Oppositions of Religious Doctrines*, London, Macmillan; New York, Herder & Herder, 1972.

Cobb J. B., *Beyond Dialogue: Towards a Mutual Transformation of Christianity and Buddhism*, Philadelphia, Fortress Press, 1982.

Congar, Y., *The Wide World My Parish*, London, Darton, Longman & Todd, 1961.

Cox H., *Turning East: The Promise and Peril of the New Orientalism*, Harmondsworth, Penguin, 1977.

Cracknell K., *Towards a New Relationship: Christians and People of Other Faiths*, London, Epworth Press, 1986.

Cragg K., *The Call of the Minaret*, New York, Oxford University Press, 1965.

The Christian and Other Religions, London, Mowbray, 1977.

Muhammad and the Christian: A Question of Response, London, Darton, Longman & Todd; Maryknoll, NY, Orbis, 1984.

Sandals at the Mosque, London, SCM, 1959.

Davis C., *Christ and the World Religions*, London, Hodder & Stoughton, 1970.

Davis S. (ed.), *Encountering Evil*, Edinburgh, T. & T. Clark, 1981.

D'Costa G., *Christianity and the Encounter with Other Religions: A Bibliographical Guide*, London, 1987.

Dewick E. C., *The Christian Attitude to Other Religions*, Cambridge, Cambridge University Press, 1953.

Dharmasiri G., *A Buddhist Critique of the Christian Concept of God*, Colombo, Sri Lanka, Lake House Institute, 1974.

Dhavamony M. (ed.), *Evangelism, Dialogue and Development*, Rome, Universitie Gregoriana Editrice, 1972.

Doumlin H., *Christianity Meets Buddhism*, La Salle, Ill., Open Court, 1974.

Drummond R. H., *Gautama the Buddha: An Essay in Religious Understanding*, Grand Rapids, Michigan, Eerdmans Publishing, 1974.

Eminyan M., *The Theology of Salvation*, Boston, Mass., St. Paul's Publications, 1960.

Ernst C., *Multiple Echo*, London, Darton, Longman & Todd, 1979.

Farquhar J. N., *The Crown of Hinduism*, Oxford, Oxford University Press, 1930.

Flannery A. (ed.), *The Conciliar and Post-Conciliar Documents* (Vatican II Documents), Leominster, Fowler Wright, 1975.

George S., *Gandhi's Challenge to Christianity*, London, Allen & Unwin, 1939.

Goulder M. (ed.), *Incarnation and Myth: The Debate Continued*, London, SCM, 1979.

Graham A., *Zen Catholicism: A Suggestion*, New York, Harcourt Brace, 1963.

Griffiths B., *The Marriage of East and West*, London, Collins, 1982.

Return to the Centre, London, Collins, 1978.

Hacker P., *Theological Foundations of Evangelization*, St Augustin, Steyler Verlag, 1980.

Hallencreutz C. F., *From Kraemer Towards Tambaram: A Study in*

Hendrik Kraemer's Missionary Approach, Lund, CWK Gleerups, 1966.

New Approaches to Men of Other Faiths, 1938–1968: A Theological Discussion, Geneva, WCC, 1970.

Hick J.

Books

Death and Eternal Life, London, Collins/Fount, 1976.

Faith and Knowledge, 2nd edn., London, Collins/Fount, 1978.

God has Many Names, London, Macmillan, 1980; US edn, Philadelphia, Westminster Press, 1982.

God and the Universe of Faiths, London, Collins/Fount, 1977.

(ed.), *The Myth of God Incarnate*, London, SCM, 1977.

The Philosophy of Religion, Englewood Cliffs, NJ, Prentice Hall, 1964; 2nd edn, 1973; 3rd edn, 1983.

(ed.), *Truth and Dialogue*, London, Sheldon Press, 1974.

The Second Christianity, London, SCM, 1983.

in Davis S. (ed.), *Encountering Evil*, Edinburgh, T. & T. Clark, 1981.

in Goulder M. (ed.), *Incarnation and Myth: The Debate Continued*, London, SCM, 1979.

in Smith W., *The Meaning and End of Religion: A New Approach to the Religious Traditions of Mankind*, London, SPCK, 1978, foreword, pp. ix–xviii.

in Whaling F. (ed.), *The World's Religious Traditions: Current Perspectives in Religious Studies*, Edinburgh, T. & T. Clark, 1984.

and Askari H. (eds), *The Experience of Religious Diversity*, Gower, Aldershot, 1985.

and Goulder M., *Why Believe in God?*, London, SCM, 1983.

Articles

'On conflicting truth claims', *Religious Studies*, 19 (1983), pp. 485–91.

'On grading religions', *Religious Studies*, 17 (1981), pp. 451–69.

'Pluralism and the reality of the transcendent', *Christian Century*, 98 (1981), pp. 45–8.

'The theology of religious pluralism', *Theology*, 86 (1983), pp. 335–40.

Hillman E., *Polygamy Reconsidered*, Maryknoll, NY, Orbis, 1975.

The Wider Ecumenism: Anonymous Christianity and the Church, London, Burns & Oates; New York, Herder & Herder, 1968.

Hocking W. E., *Living Religions and a World Faith*, London, Allen & Unwin; New York, Macmillan, 1940.

Re-thinking Missions, New York, Harper & Row, 1932.

Hoekstra H., *Evangelism in Eclipse*, Exeter, Paternoster, 1979.

Hogg W. R., *Ecumenical Foundations: A History of the International Missionary Council and its Nineteenth Century Background*, New York, Harper & Row, 1952.

Horner N. (ed.), *Protestant Currents in Mission: The Ecumenical–Conservative Encounter*, Nashville, Tenn., Abingdon, 1968.

Jathanna E. O., *The Decisiveness of the Christ–Event*, Berne, P. Lang, 1981.

Johnston W., *Christian Zen*, New York, Harper & Row, 1971.
Silent Music, New York, Harper & Row; London, Collins, 1974.
The Still Point: Reflections on Zen and Christian Mysticism, New York, Fordham University Press, 1970.

Klein C., *Anti-Judaism in Christian Theology*, Philadelphia, Fortress Press; London, SPCK, 1978.

Klostermaier K., *Hindu and Christian in Vrindaban*, London, SCM, 1969.
Kristvidya, Bangalore, CLS, 1967.

Knitter P., *No Other Name? A Critical Study of Christian Attitudes Towards the World Religions*, London, SCM, 1985.

Kraemer H.

The Christian Message in a Non-Christian World, London, Edinburgh House Press, 1938.
The Communication of the Christian Faith, London, Lutterworth Press, 1957.
Religion and the Christian Faith, London, Lutterworth Press, 1956.
Why Christianity of All Religions?, London, Lutterworth Press, 1962.
World Cultures and World Religions, London, Lutterworth Press, 1960.
in Paton W. (ed.), *The Authority of Faith*, London, Humphrey Milford/Oxford, Oxford University Press (Tambaram Series 1), 1939.

Kulandran S., *Grace: A Comparative Study of the Doctrine in Christianity and Hinduism*, London, Lutterworth Press, 1964.

Küng H., *On Being a Christian*, New York, Doubleday; London, Collins, 1976.

Lamb C., *Belief in a Mixed Society*, London, Lion, 1985.

Langley M., *Ethical Dialogue with Other Religions*, Bramcote, Grove Books, 1979.

Lausanne Committee for World Evangelization, *How Shall They Hear? Proceedings and Reports from the Consultation of World Evangelization*, Minneapolis, World Wide Publications, 1981.

Lewis H. D., *Jesus in the Faith of Christians*, London, Macmillan, 1981.

Lindbeck G., *The Nature of Doctrine: Religion and Theology in a Postliberal Age*, London, SPCK, 1984.

Lombardi R., *The Salvation of the Unbeliever*, London, Burns & Oates, 1956.

Lubac H. de, *The Church: Paradox and Mystery*, Shannon, Ireland, Ecclesia Press, 1969.

Mattam J., *Land of the Trinity: A Study of Modern Christian Approaches to Hinduism*, Bangalore, Theological Publications of India, 1975.

Maurice F. D., *The Religions of the World and their Relations to Christianity* (Boyle Lectures), London, Macmillan, 1886.

Merton T., *Zen and the Birds of Appetite*, New York, New Directions, 1968.

Moltmann J., *The Church in the Power of the Spirit*, London SCM; New York, Harper & Row, 1977.

Monchanin J. (Weber J. ed.), *In Quest of the Absolute. The Life and Works of Jules Monchanin*, Oxford, Mowbrays, 1977.

Neill S., *Christian Faith and Other Faiths: The Christian Dialogue with Other Religions*, Oxford, Oxford University Press, 1970.

Crises of Belief (rev. edn), London, Hodder & Stoughton, 1984.

A History of the Church: Christian Missions, Harmondsworth, Penguin, 1964.

Neuner J. (ed.), *Christian Revelation and World Religions*, London, Burns & Oates, 1967.

Newbigin L., *Christian Witness in a Plural Society*, London, BCC, 1977.

The Finality of Christ, London, SCM; Atlanta, Ga, John Knox Press, 1969.

The Open Secret, New York, Eerdmans Publishing, 1978.

Otto R., *India's Religion of Grace and Christianity Compared and Contrasted*, New York, Macmillan, 1930.

Pailin D., *Attitudes to Other Religions: Comparative Religion in Seventeenth and Eighteenth Century Britain*, Manchester, Manchester University Press, 1984.

Panikkar R., *The Intrareligious Dialogue*, New York, Paulist Press, 1978.

Myth, Faith and Hermeneutics, Leominster, Fowler Wright, 1979.

The Trinity and the Religious Experience of Man, London, Darton, Longman & Todd, 1973.

The Unknown Christ of Hinduism, London, Darton, Longman & Todd, 1964: rev. edn, 1981.

Pannenberg W., *Basic Questions in Theology*, vol. 2, London, SCM, 1971.

Parrinder G., *Avatar and Incarnation*, London, Faber & Faber, 1970.

Paton W. (ed.), *The Authority of Faith*, London, Humphrey Milford/ Oxford, Oxford University Press (Tambaram Series 1), 1939.

Percy E. (ed.), *Facing the Unfinished Task: Messages Delivered at the*

Congress on World Mission, Michigan, Eerdmans Publishing, 1961.

Race A., *Christians and Religious Pluralism*, London, SCM, 1983.

Rahner K.

Foundations of Christian Faith, London, Darton, Longman & Todd, 1978.
Spirit in the World, 2nd edn, London, Sheed & Ward, 1968.
Theological Investigations, vols 1–20, London, Darton, Longman & Todd; New York, Seabury Press, 1961–84.
and Thussing W., *A New Christology*, London, Burns & Oates, 1980.

Robinson J. A. T., *Truth is Two-Eyed*, London, SCM, 1979.

Rouner L. (ed.), *Religious Pluralism*, Indiana, Notre Dame University Press, 1984.

Rousseau R. W. (ed.), *Interreligious Dialogue*, Montrose, Ridge Row, 1981.

Samartha S., *Courage for Dialogue*, Geneva, WCC, 1981.
The Hindu Response to the Unbound Christ, Madras, CLS, 1974.
(ed.), *Living Faiths and Ultimate Goals*, Geneva, WCC, 1974.
(ed.), *Towards World Community: Resources and Responsibilities for Living Together* (Colombo Papers), Geneva, WCC, 1975.

Schlette H. R., *Towards a Theology of Religions*, 'Questiones Disputate' Series, London, Burns & Oates, 1966.

Sharpe E., *Comparative Religion: A History*, London, Duckworth, 1975.
Faith Meets Faith: Some Christian Attitudes to Hinduism in the Nineteenth and Twentieth Centuries, London, SCM, 1977.
Not to Destroy But to Fulfil: The Contribution of J. N. Farquhar to Protestant Missionary Thought in India Before 1914, Lund, CWK Gleerups, 1965.

Shorter A., *African Culture and the Christian Church*, London, Geoffrey Chapman, 1973.

Smart N., *Beyond Ideology*, New York, Harper & Row, 1981.
The Yogi and the Devotee: The Interplay between the Upanishads and Catholic Theology, London, Allen & Unwin, 1968.

Smith W. C., *The Faith of Other Men*, New York, Harper Torchbooks, 1972.
The Meaning and End of Religion: A New Approach to the Religious Traditions of Mankind, New York, Harper & Row, 1962; London, SPCK, 2nd edn, 1978.
Towards a World Theology, London, Macmillan, 1980.

SNC, *Guidelines for a Dialogue between Christians and Muslims*, Rome, SNC, 1969.

Religions: Fundamental Themes for a Dialogistic Understanding, Rome, SNC, 1970.

Straelen H. van, *The Catholic Encounter with World Religions*, London, Burns & Oates; New York, Newman Press, 1966.

Tambaram-Madras Series: International Missionary Council Meeting, vol. 1, Oxford, Oxford University Press, 1939.

Thomas M. M., *The Acknowledged Christ of the Indian Renaissance*, London, SCM, 1969.

Thomas O. C. (ed.), *Attitudes Towards Other Religions*, London, SCM, 1969.

Thussing W., *A New Christology*, London, Burns & Oates, 1980.

Tillich P., *Christianity and the Encounter of the World Religions*, New York, Columbia University Press, 1963.

Toynbee A., *Christianity Among the Religions of the World*, New York, Scribners, 1957.

Troeltsch E., *The Absoluteness of Christianity*, London, SCM, 1972; Atlanta, Ga, John Knox Press, 1981.

Christian Thought: Its History and Application, New York, Meridian; London, University of London Press, 1957.

Vandana Sr, *Social Justice and Ashrams*, Bangalore, Asian Trading Corporation, 1982.

Vatican II Documents, see Flannery A. (ed.).

Visser't Hooft W., *No Other Name: The Choice Between Syncretism and Universalism*, London, SCM, 1963.

Warren M., *Social History and Christian Mission*, London, SCM, 1967.

WCC, *Guidelines on Dialogue With People of Living Faiths and Ideologies*, Geneva, WCC, 1979.

Weber J., see Monchanin J.

Whaling F. (ed.), *The World's Religious Traditions: Current Perspectives in Religious Studies*, Edinburgh, T. & T. Clark, 1984.

Zaehner R. C., *At Sundry Times*, London, Faber & Faber, 1958.

The Concordant Discord, Oxford, Oxford University Press, 1970.

ADDITIONAL WORKS

Aquinas T., *De Veritate Catholicae Fidei* (Pegis A. ed.), Indiana, Notre Dame University Press, 1975.

Summa Theologiae, I–II (Gilby T. ed.), London, Blackfriars, 1964.

Bacik J., *Apologetics and the Eclipse of Mystery – Mystagogy According to Karl Rahner*, Indiana and London, Notre Dame University Press, 1980.

Baillie D. and Martin H. (eds), *Revelation*, London, Faber & Faber, 1937.

Balthasar H. von, *The Moment of Christian Witness*, New York, Newman Press, 1969.

Boros L., *The Moment of Truth*, London, Burns & Oates, 1965.

Braaten C., *The Future of God*, New York, Herder & Herder, 1969.

Braithwaite R., *An Empiricist's View of the Nature of Religious Belief*, Cambridge, Cambridge University Press, 1955.

Buber M., *Between Man and Man*, London, Kegan & Paul, 1947.

Carpenter J., *Theism in Medieval India*, London, William Wargate, 1921.

Cox H., *The Secular City*, London, Pelican, 1965.

Cragg G., *The Church and the Age of Reason: 1648–1798*, Harmondsworth, Penguin, 1983.

Cupitt D., *Taking Leave of God*, London, SCM, 1980.

The World to Come, London, SCM, 1982.

Denzinger H., *The Sources of Catholic Dogma*, London, Herder & Herder, 1957.

Dhavamony M., *Love of God According to Saiva Siddhanta*, Oxford, Oxford University Press, 1971.

Dulles A., *Models of the Church: A Critical Assessment of the Church in All Its Aspects*, London, Macmillan, 1976.

The Resilient Church: The Necessity and Limits of Adaptation, New York, Doubleday, 1977.

Dunn J. G., *Christology in the Making*, London, SCM, 1980.

Eliot T. S., *Collected Poems*, London, Faber & Faber, 1963.

Ellwood R., *Alternative Altars: Unconventional and Eastern Spirituality in America*, Chicago, Ill., Chicago University Press, 1979.

Garaudy R. (ed.), *From Anathema to Dialogue*, London, Collins, 1967.

Gombrich R., *Precept and Practice*, Oxford, Oxford University Press, 1971.

Green M. (ed.), *The Truth of God Incarnate*, London, Hodder & Stoughton, 1977.

Gutierrez G., *A Theology of Liberation: History, Politics and Salvation*, London, SCM, 1974.

Hacker P., *Kleine Schriften*, Wiesbaden, Franz Steiner Verlag GmbH, 1978.

Hogg A., *Towards Clarifying My Reactions to Doctor Kraemer's Book*, Madras, Diocesan Press, 1938.

Hulmes E., *Commitment and Neutrality in Religious Education*, London, Geoffrey Chapman, 1979.

Hume D., *Dialogues Concerning Natural Religion* (Pike N. ed.), Indiana, Bobbs-Meril, 1970.

James W., *The Varieties of Religious Experience*, London, Collins/Fount, 1977.

Kopf D., *British Orientalism and the Bengal Renaissance: The Dynamics of Indian Modernization 1773–1835*, Los Angeles, University of California Press, 1969.

Kristen B., *The Meaning of Religion: Lectures in the Phenomenology of Religion*, The Hague, Martinus Nijhoff, 1960.

Kuhn T., *The Structure of Scientific Revolutions*, Chicago, Ill., Chicago University Press, 1970.

Küng H., *The Church*, London, Search Press, 1968.

Lash N., *Theology on Dover Beach*, London, Darton, Longman & Todd, 1979.

Leeuwen A. Th. van, *Henrik Kraemer: Dienaar der Wereldkerke*, Amsterdam, ten Have, 1959.

Ling T., *A History of Religion East and West*, London, Macmillan, 1968.

McBrien R., *Catholicism*, London, Geoffrey Chapman, 1980.

Mascall E., *Existence and Analogy*, London, Longman, Green, 1949.

Minear P., *Images of the Church in the New Testament*, Philadelphia, Fortress Press, 1960.

Moule C., *The Origins of Christology*, Cambridge, Cambridge University Press, 1977.

Newman J., *An Essay on the Development of Christian Doctrine*, London, Longmans, Green, 1906.

Norman E. R., *Christianity and the World Order*, Oxford, Oxford University Press, 1979.

Rad G. von, *The Message of the Prophets*, London, SCM, 1968.

Radhakrishnan S., *A Hindu View of Life*, London, George Allen & Unwin, 1927.

Rayapati J. R., *Early American Interest in Vedanta*, London, Asian Publishing House, 1973.

Riches J., *The Analogy of Beauty*, Edinburgh, T. & T. Clark, 1986.

Robinson T. H., *Prophecy and Prophets in Ancient Israel*, London, SCM, 1953.

Schillebeeckx E., *Jesus: An Experiment in Christology*, London, Collins, 1979.

Smart N., *The Phenomenon of Religion*, London, Mowbrays, 1978.
The Religious Experience of Mankind, London, Collins, 1977.

Smart N. and Horder D. (eds), *New Movements in Religious Education*, London, Temple Smith, 1975.

Tillich P., *What is Religion?*, New York, Harper & Row, 1969.

Tracy D., *The Analogical Imagination*, London, SCM, 1981.

Vorgrimler H., *Karl Rahner: His Life, Thought and Works*, London, Burns & Oates, 1965.

Wedberg A., *A History of Philosophy*, vol. 2, Oxford, Oxford University Press, 1982.

Weger H., *Karl Rahner: An Introduction to His Theology*, London, Burns & Oates, 1980.

Wittgenstein L., *Philosophical Investigations*, Oxford, Basil Blackwell, 1958.

Index